STRANGERS & ALIENS

AN ANECDOTAL COMMENTARY on 1 PETER

TREY DUNHAM

ISBN: **1484036409**
ISBN-13: **978-1484036402**

DEDICATION

To my beautiful Grace.
This journey wouldn't be the same without you.

CONTENTS

ACKNOWLEDGMENTS

As much as we fight it, who we are and what we do with our lives is affected greatly by our family. My father, himself a writer, has been encouraging me to write a book for years, which I always thought was odd, because I didn't think I had anything interesting to share. Then it dawned on me that my family is pretty unusual and strange and wonderful and interesting. And the Bible has always fascinated me, so it seemed like a good idea to try to bring the two together somehow.

This book is largely a story about them, about us, and the journey we have shared so far. So thank you, my sweet Grace, Mom and Dad, Tim/Tad, Jon and Joe for the adventure. I couldn't imagine a better group of weirdos to have been begat from. Thank you, Jill and Anna, for being such great wives to my brothers and for putting up with a lot. Thanks to all my great nieces and nephews: Sam, Anna, Andy, Canaan, Ruth and Jonah. You all are so much fun and full of life. I can't wait to see where God takes you!

While I grew up in Wyoming, Morgantown, WV has become my home, largely because of the great community of friends that have accepted me here. It would be ridiculous to try to name everyone so I won't, but I do have to mention a couple folks. Mark and Lauren, your bountiful friendship (not to mention dinner table) has changed my life. Thank you for supporting me and standing with me through some of the toughest and best years of my life. And thank you, Brent, for your friendship and the many long spiritual discussions at Peking House and beyond. I so appreciate your encouragement for me to write, and the original suggestion that we study 1 Peter at cityChurch.

When I left my last job, I didn't know what God had in store for me, but I could have hardly wanted for a more loving, generous, kind, patient and wonderful community than the one that God has brought together these past three years. I have been sharpened by each one of you.

Also a huge thank you to my editor, Lauren. I knew I had the right person when I found out you read grammar books for fun. You have been a great supporter and the work you have done is incredible. Thank you.

And finally, thanks to Peter, who through the Holy Spirit has written an amazing book that has changed my view of God, others and the course and tenor of my spiritual journey. This book wouldn't exist without yours. And I can't wait to meet you.

TREY DUNHAM

INTRODUCTION

My daughter has always wanted to go to Paris. Or Canada. I think in her nine-year old mind they are equally exotic and foreign. She also has trips in the works to China, Japan, Africa, South America and New York. We talk often about what those places must be like, the food, the smells in the air, the people. We imagine ourselves walking down the tree-lined Champs Elysees in Paris or climbing the rough and uneven stairs on the Great Wall or hiking the path to Machu Picchu in Peru.

Hardly a week goes by she doesn't remind me how excited she is to go on our next trip.

I understand that part of her fascination with foreign lands comes from me and my upbringing. My parents grew up in rural Michigan and really did very little traveling as kids. Of course the '40s and '50s were a different time, before globalization. It was just more difficult to get around in those days. And being the daughter of a farmer and the son of a printer, time and money were issues.

My mom recalls one trip she took across the country. Her mother, father, brother and sister set out after harvest in the fall in a huge old Packard toward California. She said they took their school books with them and studied as they toured the mountains of the West, Yellowstone and the Tetons. They saw the Pacific coast of Oregon and California, the hot, dry plains of Texas and the soupy humidity of the Deep South wedged in the backseat of that car.

And that was that. I don't know that there was ever another trip. The farm kept them busy and at home. Mom never said she regretted this as a child, but I am sure she thought of what other places and sites there must be to see.

I am not sure my father ever went very far with his family. Growing up in small town, his parents, having lived through the Depression, did not think travel and sightseeing were things one needed to spend money on.

But Dad moved to Ohio, then New York, then California for college and graduate school, an expanding circle of places, people and experiences opening up like a new book, the binding creaking and protesting a bit, pages stiff and sore like unused limbs just waking up. There was a whole world out there--places equally fascinating and frightening, intriguing and intimidating. But he was hooked. He wanted to go everywhere, see everything.

I am sure my parents did not miss traveling when they were young. Indeed, they didn't know any better. It is hard to miss what you don't know. But the few experiences they did have started to grow in them a love for other countries, for exploring new places.

And I think that took root in me and then in my daughter. I do not know what that seed is, how it gets planted or why some get it and others do not, but I do have a thing for the road.

In college, my younger brother Tim and I had an 1967 Volkswagen bus, complete with a wood-paneled interior, that we would drive from our home in Wyoming to school in Ohio. That poor bus couldn't reach more than 56 or 57 miles per hour max, but it didn't matter to us.

Tim and I would take turns driving--a tank of gas then we would switch and sit in the bean bag in the back, rest, and watch the land change from the soft yellows and browns of the west to the lush greens of the east. There is hardly anything better than the windows down, sun shining, motoring across central Nebraska, blasting U2's *Joshua Tree* on the stereo. Some of my happiest days have been on the road.

I think I was made a traveler. I do not know if it is something that is innate in me or something that I learned from my parents, but I think something in me has been unhinged. Something that makes it difficult for me to stay put, to stay at home for a very long time. Sometimes when I get a bit depressed or on edge, my friend Lauren will tell me I need to go on a trip somewhere.

But I also wonder if we all aren't somehow born with the need to see and explore and experience new places. I understand it is a more robust inclination in some than others. But maybe this is just a symptom of circumstance and upbringing. Maybe if we all had the chance or a parent or a friend who would take us to Paris or Canada or California or wherever we would discover something about ourselves, about the way we were made, about the traveler in us all.

Why Do I Feel So Strange?

When I was in junior high I was invited to my first New Year's Eve party. It was in the home, the basement to be exact, of Staci Williams' house. Staci Williams was a ninth grader, popular by all accounts, a cheerleader (of course) and generally considered on the A-list at Laramie Junior High School. The party was for her ninth- grade friends, mostly A's and maybe a B-lister sprinkler in here and there.

I, on the other hand, was the only eighth grader in the room which gave me an immediate social ranking of C minus to, more realistically, D plus. The only reason I made the cut was because I was staying with Brad Deaton (an obvious A-lister with his bleach-tipped/frosted hair and Coca-Cola rugby shirt) and his family over the holiday. And I was staying with them because my parents were in Europe and Brad's dad and my dad worked together.

I think Brad felt sorry for me, so he let me tag along.

I have never felt very comfortable at parties. Small dinner parties with good friends are nice, but get me in a crowd that is loud and crazy and I retreat to the nearest wall and/or corner. I am content to watch. I sat the entire party on a couch next to the TV. I literally did not move from that spot for four hours. And I really had to go to the bathroom.

Someone once told me that I am an extroverted introvert. Get me on a stage in front of a couple thousand people and I will tell story after story. The stage provides a wonderful distance.

Get me in a room with strangers and I drift toward the wall, like a timid ice skater grabbing and pulling his way around the edge of the rink, trying to stay out of the way.

Maybe my awkwardness, my reticence, is not outwardly evident, but inside I feel like I am in the wrong place.

But I think my discomfort goes beyond just social settings. Most of the time I feel out of place, like I don't really fit in. I am not talking about the feeling of being unwelcome or ostracized; this is something totally different. This is more of a sense of uneasiness, like the feeling you get when you are looking for something. I feel like I am looking for myself sometimes.

The other day I left my phone at home. I use my phone pretty much constantly all day for email, texting, phone calls, calendar, reminders, Facebook, Twitter, checking sports' scores and the weather, taking pictures. I felt very unbalanced and out of whack that whole day. As if a piece of me was missing.

That is the kind of feeling I am talking about, like I don't fit in because something about me is missing and I can't find it or get to it for some reason. There is an uneasiness to that, an unrest.

I wonder if this is why I like to travel; maybe I am looking for my real home and I have not yet been able to find it or get there.

Travel seems to be mostly about going to look for something we do not have: a place, a site, a cathedral or historical landmark, an experience of adventure or rest and relaxation. Travel is at its root about the pursuit of something we do not have or something we have not seen. It is a lot about trying to fill in a gap, a hole in our life, trying to find something that we think or feel may be missing.

If we had nothing to look for or felt no sense of missing out or of something lost (or potentially lost) we would have no need to move. We would stay at home, perfectly content.

C.S. Lewis wrote, "If I find in myself a desire which no experience in this world can satisfy, the most probable explanation is that I was made for another world."

This makes a lot of sense to me because I realize that I have not experienced everything, that there are still places to go and people to meet and understand. I am not yet a whole person and that motivates, indeed, compels me to move, to search, to go. But I have a suspicion that whatever it is that unseats me, that thing that awakens in me an uneasiness, may not be, as Lewis suggests, in this world, but another.

And that the reason I feel out of place is because I am not at home. I am a stranger and an alien in this place, and we will all always feel unrest until we find our way home.

When I was in college I took a Great Books class and Dr. Kliska made us read Augustine's *Confessions*. I remember two things from that book: first, Augustine wondering at himself when he, as a young man, stole some apples from a neighbor when he was not hungry and did not need them. He went on for about ten pages about his motives and all that. I could have told him the problem in a sentence. You're a punk, Augustine! Philosophers.

The other thing I remember is what he said about feeling uncomfortable and out of place in the world. He wrote, "Our hearts are restless, until they find their rest in You."

The "You" he was talking about is God.

Over the years, this short quote from a very old book has served as a kind of guide for me. When I feel out of place, when I feel unsure of where I am going, when my heart feels restless, I remember Augustine. I remember his simple observation, grown out of decades of experience and searching and of his own travel. I connect with him as one connects with others who share the same fate, the weight of restlessness, of wandering. It is the weight of being a foreigner and an outlander looking for home.

I am thankful for men like Augustine and Lewis, because they have, in their brief observations, given me some direction, a general point from which I can orient myself and launch out into the unfamiliar, the unknown. Like the needle of a compass that tells you which way to go, they point me in the direction of home.

We Need a Map

I hate to admit it, but for someone who loves to travel I have a pretty bad sense of direction. I routinely head out with full confidence that I am going the right way, only to figure out an hour later that I have no idea where I am.

I think I get it from my mother who, dear and kind as she is, would get lost on her way to the grocery store. And this in a town she and my father had lived for three years. She also drove for over an hour in the wrong direction after getting back onto the highway after a rest stop.

My brother Tim on the other hand is like a human compass. We could emerge from a subway in the middle of a foreign city at midnight and he would immediately chart the exact course we needed to take in about two seconds. I would still be looking at my watch and simultaneously trying to locate the sun's quadrant and calculate the angle of Orion's belt respective to the equator and then inverting that to compensate for the fact we were 20 degrees into the southern hemisphere.

Eventually, I just swallowed my pride and followed him, occasionally offering," I think it's this way."

To which he would reply, pointing in the exact opposite direction, "No, it's this way."

I wonder if Magellan had an annoying older brother trying his best to get them lost.

As irritating as it was to always think I knew the right direction only to be corrected, I was really thankful that Tim was around to keep me on the right path. Any traveler worth their salt knows they need a guide from time to time.

When Grace and I went camping in Canada last summer, we took a map. Well, a road atlas and a GPS. We used the map to help us see the big picture. We would lay out the atlas on our picnic table at our campsite and see the general route we wanted to take around the St. Lawrence waterway from Niagara Falls and on into Ontario, Quebec and New Brunswick, then back into Maine and down through New York and Pennsylvania before coming home to West Virginia. Each night we would look at that atlas for the next provincial or national park that was about a half day's drive from where we were.

It was really comforting to see where we were going, to see the roads, in blue and red, laying there on the paper waiting for us, marking the path that would eventually lead us home, but also lead us to some incredible new and beautiful places we had never seen before. This atlas would guide us into some challenging places, a raging thunderstorm high on a cliff overlooking Lake Ontario and some of the most meaningful times like when Grace and I canoed together in silence through the grand mountainous network of lakes in St. Mauricie National Park.

I loved that atlas because it gave me some perspective, helped me understand in some way where I was going and helped me to eventually get home.

It is probably cliché to say that life is a journey. Many books have been written following that line of thought, about a myriad of different people going a million different ways through life.

And I am sure it would not surprise you if I were to tell you that this, too, is a book about a journey, my spiritual journey, or parts of it at least, because it would be impossible to tell everything there is to tell.

But I think that this book is unique because it follows, as its guide, the first letter of the Apostle Peter. It is a commentary of sorts in that it follows the trajectory of the book from beginning to end, but not in the traditional sense of chapter by chapter, verse by verse explanation and exposition. Rather, I have found 1 Peter to be more of a spiritual map or guidebook that can, if we refer to it, follow it, lead us through this life and into the next.

I didn't so much choose 1 Peter as it chose me. Our church started studying through the book about two years ago, and as we did, I began to realize how much it spoke to my own experience, how Peter's words mirrored and related to the course God had brought me on over the years. It has helped me to make sense of my experience in a new and practical way.

Little passages and thoughts jumped out at me and I thought, "That is exactly what I went through!" or "That is just how I felt that one time!" and "That is a really good and practical thought! Nice work, Peter!"

I think the Bible speaks to us like that. I really do think it is, as Paul says, "living and active" and that it is "useful" for teaching, correcting, encouraging and guiding us in life. And so not only has 1 Peter been revelatory and descriptive in helping me to understand my experience, but also *practical* and *prescriptive* as it lays out a course of action for those looking.

And I think you will be surprised by Peter, that his ancient writings from thousands of years ago could have something relevant to say to you today. I think you might be surprised by his depth of insight and that maybe he can help you figure out some things about this journey you are on.

As this is a commentary of sorts, I think I should mention a couple things about my methodology. I will be the first to acknowledge that it is far from rigorous, and the theologians among us will no doubt have much to say about that.

Instead I took a layman's approach, asking first, what is Peter trying to say? This is a letter after all, so it only makes sense that he would have an intent, something he is trying to communicate. And with Peter being an uneducated man, my supposition is that it isn't going to take a rocket scientist to decipher that message. So, what is the plain and straightforward message from Peter?

Second, I believe that this particular writing had another author, God Himself through the Holy Spirit, and so I sought to understand His message for me, trusting that He would highlight the important points, ideas, thoughts, actions steps, etc. that He wanted me to get.

An inexact science to be sure, but I trust that God loves His Word and message more than I do and He is fully capable of bringing the important bits to life and to my attention as I read.

And I hope God will do the same for you. Before you begin reading my thoughts on 1 Peter, I hope that you will take a few moments, or a day or two to read through the letter for yourself, paying special attention to what you think Peter was talking about and even more, those bits that God, through the Holy Spirit, highlights in your mind.

Write your observations down, write about why you think a particular idea or thought jumped out at you. How does this relate to your life in the past? And how might it change your course going forward?

I hope you will try this exercise. It is far better for you to read and study and know God through the Bible than for you to read my commentary. But once you are done, I am excited to share my journey, my thoughts, my observations from 1 Peter with you.

JOIN THE CONVERSATION

Before you read the next chapter stop and read 1 Peter 1:1-5 and share what you think on Twitter at #Strangers&Aliens. I'd love to talk about what jumps out at you.

1 BEING A TOURIST
1 Peter 1:1-5

The first time I went to another country I was 11 years old. My father had taken a sabbatical from the University of Wyoming for a year to do research in the jungles of Papua New Guinea and teach kids how to shoot free throws (more on this later, it's a long story)--but this was really just a front. What he really wanted to do was travel.

I can still remember the day he came home and told us to pack our bags. "We are heading to New Guinea!" We were at the dinner table, my three brothers, my mother and I, mouths agape, little pieces of chuckwagon roundup (a lovely dish my mother would make consisting of corn bread, baked beans and hot dogs) dangling from our lips. We were dumbstruck, but he seemed to have it all figured out:

"First we will head to Europe, then hop on over to Greece, Sri Lanka and Singapore, hit New Guinea for about eight months, then head home through the Philippines, Taiwan, China and Japan."

Actually, I am pretty sure he didn't have all the details worked out at that point. A lot of it had to be figured out and arranged on the way. I distinctly remember being stuck in Athens for about a week while Mom and Dad negotiated with a travel agent for the best price out of there.

But the point was clear: we were leaving to go on the road. My dad, my mom and four blond-haired, blue-eyed boys, ages 4-11.

"Can we finish dinner first?" my mother calmly replied.

9

My brothers and I were too young and inexperienced in the world to really understand the hardship, danger and expense of what my father was suggesting. We were just excited. Mom and Dad bought us all matching backpacks that we would use for our trip around the world. He handed them to us with the manifesto, "If you can't carry it, you can't bring it." I am not sure if he meant this to apply to four-year old Joe, but we all took him very seriously.

I had a recurring dream in the months leading up to our trip. I was in the deep bush of New Guinea, leading an expedition to our new home. The traveling party, which consisted mostly of my family, cowered behind me, looking very scared, confused and crying softly as I slashed through the thick jungle undergrowth, blazing a trail where no person had ever been before.

I, of course, was wearing a sharp adventurer's outfit complete with leather boots, cargo pants, one of those safari-type shirts with all the pockets, and a brimmed hat like Indiana Jones. Strapped to my side was a ten-inch Bowie knife and a bullwhip. In my hand, a full-sized machete, wielded with all the skill of King Arthur or Braveheart himself.

The dream always ended the same way: a giant snake would fall onto me from the canopy. Wrapping its muscular coils around me one at a time, I would awaken just as my grasping hand found the Bowie knife.

Pretty exciting stuff.

But I had no idea. New Guinea was actually nothing like my dream, although there were some pretty large snakes, dense jungles and sharp knives with which I about cut off my finger. But that is another story.

While my dream was way off, I realize now that this trip awakened some things in me. I think that I started to see the world in a new way, even before we left. I began to imagine what was possible, what else was out there. Just the thought of going to another country had provoked me to think differently, to consider different ways of looking at the world.

Anyone who has traveled can tell you that being in unfamiliar surroundings, you start to notice and see things that you didn't see before. You have new angles and perspectives.

There are certain of your senses that are heightened when you are are away from home. When you step outside your normal sphere of existence, whether it be into another city, another state or another country, your perceptions and sensibilities change, and things you do not normally think about push their way to the front of your mind.

It is really interesting to me that Peter begins his first letter, "to God's elect, strangers in the world...." (1:1) That is not a normal way to start a letter. I don't think any of the other epistles in the Bible kick off anything like that. Paul usually opens with something kind of sentimental, like "To Timothy, my dear son," or encouraging, "To those sanctified in Christ Jesus...."

To call them strangers just seems a little weird to me. The word literally means to live somewhere as a foreigner or a tourist, which may have seemed odd to them. In those days, people were less mobile. Few people traveled as it was difficult and dangerous and the idea of tourism or a vacation was not really part of the culture at that time. I am sure they were all living pretty much where they had lived their whole lives.

I imagine them asking, "Why is Peter calling us foreigners, he has our address, how else could he have mailed us this letter?" They must have been a little confused; perhaps not unlike the Dunham family, sitting around that dinner table listening to our father describe the adventures we were about to have, the whole new world we would experience, the things we would see and who we would become as people. I think every last one of us around that table was wondering, "What in the world is he talking about?"

In my understanding, Peter wants to be clear from the very beginning that we are on a trip; we are not at home. I think he is trying to awaken them and us to a new life, to help us all understand that because we are not home, because we are strangers, things are different for us. Or at least they should be.

There is just something that happens to you when all of a sudden, you find yourself to be a foreigner in a foreign land.

When you are at home you sometimes lose this sense of journey, that you are going somewhere, that your life has a destination and you have not yet arrived. We also often fail to look at trials, difficulties and roadblocks as part of the adventure. And I think at times our sense of curiosity, wonder and hope gets dulled, and if we're not careful we fall into thinking that this is just how it's always going to be.

But this is not the life of a traveler. Far from it.

Strangers in the World *(1 Peter 1:1-2)*

While the official language of New Guinea is English, over 700 distinct languages are spoken among the various tribes and people groups on the island. That's more than any other country in the world. In those days, as they were beginning to develop a national identity (they had just become independent from Australia in the mid 1970s), most people did business in Pidgin, a mixture of Dutch and English that you could kind of understand, but not really.

"Go naw, kisim dispela stik." Translated, "Go and get that stick." This was the one phrase my father was able to master in our year on the island, and he used it tirelessly with his four sons. Needless to say it was a long year. And we had a lot of extra firewood laying around. Not to mention weird because we all spoke pretty good English. Pretty well English. Whatever.

Stepping into another culture, language is usually the first clue that you are an outsider. I would sit around the fire listening to our friends from the village speak in their native tongue, amazed at the beauty of the words flowing between them, wishing I could enter in and understand what they were discussing with such eloquence and passion. Our words seemed so awkward and harsh in comparison.

There are other things that clue you in to the fact that you are an outsider: the food, the clothes, the housing, the smells, the way everyone seems to know where they are going except you. It is one of the most clear, precise, unnerving, exhilarating feelings in the world to be a stranger. An interesting mix of both excitement and terror.

As I mentioned previously, my parents took me and my three brothers to Greece en route to New Guinea. We got off the train in Athens, and as I recall, all the boys were wearing our matching red, white and blue shirt-short ensembles just to make sure everyone noticed us and to remove any doubt we were Americans.

My father turned to me, and in his super-serious professor voice, told me not to let go of my youngest brother, Joe. "They steal little blond-haired, blue-eyed boys like him in places like this," he said with a look in his eye that told me he wasn't joking.

I probably pondered that possibility a little too long, but soon I grabbed him tightly, a bit scared. I remember thinking, "What kind of place is it where people steal little boys? This isn't like home."

Nothing against Greece, mind you. There are bad people everywhere including the United States and unfortunately children get kidnapped all over the world all the time. The point my father was making was simply that we stick out here. People can easily see that we do not belong, we don't know how things work like the folks from here do, and that makes it much easier to take advantage of us. Because we are strangers in this land we have to be more on guard.

Of course, the longer you stay in a place the less frightened, less strange you feel. You start to blend in. About a week later, we began to realize how wonderful the Greeks were: super friendly and kind and gregarious and in love with good food and good company. I started to think I could really settle down in a place like this. They didn't even consider starting dinner until about 10 p.m. and for an 11-year old boy that makes a for a pretty appealing bedtime. Every morning we awoke to the sweet aroma the most delicious, fresh, hot doughnuts that an old man sold from a cart in the street below. Heaven.

As for my brother, I began to worry no one would actually take him, so I thought it might be a good tactic to push him out a few feet in front of me with a sign around his neck: "Free Kid. Annoying. Rarely Bites." Didn't work, but I tried.

I like it that Peter starts his first letter to the churches by calling them strangers in the world (1:1). In other places he calls them aliens (2:11). I think this is because he wants them to remember that really they are just tourists in a foreign land. And this is an important warning, to not forget where you come from.

I loved living in New Guinea as a kid, but I think it would have been odd if I had lost my connection with America. Even if I had stayed for the rest of my life, I would always have a connection with my birthplace. I might go so far as to say that it will always be my true earthly home.

There are things about me that will always be true because I was born in the U.S. My native language will always be English. I will always think you should drive on the right (*ergo*, correct) side of the road and that football is

13

played with an oblong ball and rarely actually touches one's feet. This is just who I am. If I had grown up in England or New Guinea for that matter, I think I would feel differently. I would *be* different.

These are not moral judgments, mind you. These are just qualities that one might even say are innate, part of my American-ness. They are some of what make me who I am. And it is not a question of being right or wrong, it is just a question of identity.

Paul reminds us in his letter of some of our strangeness, of what is different about us: we have been chosen by God, we have a special place in His heart, we have been purified by Him through Jesus' work on the cross, covered in His blood. (If being covered in blood doesn't seem a little different or strange, then I don't know what to tell you.) These qualities are part of our identity as Christians, as believers in God. They become who we are, part of our very nature.

Peter wants to remind us that our identity, even though we are travelers in a foreign land (maybe *especially* for that reason), is still rooted deeply in our relationship with God. No matter where we go, no matter in what culture or country we find ourselves, our identity, our true home, remains the same.

When you first enter a foreign land, everything is new and weird and different and it seems almost impossible to forget that this is not your home. Over time though, the strangeness begins to fade, the unfamiliar becomes familiar, what was once different now is ordinary. Eventually, you can forget where you come from.

There is an old saying that familiarity breeds contempt, but I think what's worse is a familiarity that breeds forgetfulness. When we are around something too long, when we become too familiar, things that once seemed valuable or precious fade into the background.

The staple food in New Guinea is a sweet potato called kau kau. My dad always described it to people as a regular Irish potato sprinkled with a little sugar. And I think that is a pretty good description. The typical way they were prepared was to be roasted over a bed of coals.

The first time I had kau kau I thought I had died and gone to heaven. It was so sweet and tender and just melted in your mouth. I had never tasted something so wonderful, so full of goodness. I think I actually uttered the words, "I could eat this for *every* meal!" Little did I know that was kind of how things work in the bush in New Guinea. Kau kau was pretty much on the menu for every meal: breakfast, lunch and dinner.

Now, I don't want to say that my love for kau kau diminished over the course of that year, I would just say that my appreciation for it was dulled by overexposure. I may have become too familiar. I love kau kau, but eating it for every meal made me realize I have a deep and profound love for cheeseburgers.

Being a stranger in a strange land is a good thing. There is a thrill to being different, a sense of adventure that comes with unfamiliar surroundings. But being a foreigner also grows your appreciation and desire for home. It reminds us that there is another way of doing things. Other types of food, other points of view. It broadens us. Travel tends to remind us of the good things we have left behind, waiting for our return.

Into Hope and Inheritance *(1 Peter 1:3-5)*

As I mentioned earlier, for our year in New Guinea our father allowed us each a single backpack into which we crammed all of our clothes, toiletries and any personal items we needed for an entire year. I think I had one pair of jeans, maybe a dress shirt. I definitely remember the aforementioned red, white and blue shirt-short ensemble each of us boys wore about every other day. And I probably had a toothbrush.

Our parents made us keep a journal that year, and every night we had to write down what we had done that day. We hated it, but my mother would assure us, "One day you will be glad you have all these memories."

She may yet be right, but looking through those old wire-bound notebooks it looks like all we did on our whole trip was, "Got up. Ate breakfast. Walked around. Saw some old church. Ate lunch. Rode on a train. Went to bed." This was literally every entry for our whole six weeks in Europe. I followed the letter of the law, but the spirit of keeping a journal escaped me.

I don't think I had much else in my pack that I can remember. Eleven-year old boys just don't have that much stuff I guess, and usually they could care less what they wear.

So while I don't remember and didn't care what was *in* my pack, I definitely remember what was *on* my pack.

While in London, our first stop on this trip, my brothers and I discovered that in many of the little tourist curio shops we would walk by, they sold little fabric patches that would have the name of the country and perhaps a flag or crest or something related to the history of the place. They were pretty cool little designs and we got the idea that it would be rad (it was the '80s) to try to find one from each country and then sew it onto our packs. It would serve to remind us of where we had been, but also, honestly, to try to impress others. Let them know we were kids who had been places and had places to go.

Pretty soon it was an obsession. Any interest we had in the cultural artifacts or architectural history of a place soon vanished. We just wanted to find our patch, and fast! Mom bought a little sewing kit and we would sit on the train as we moved on to the next place, awkwardly sewing, in big looping stitches, our latest destination reminder to our packs. We could hardly wait to get somewhere else and start looking for that next patch.

I still have that backpack stowed away in a trunk in the attic.

That whole experience/obsession with patches made me realize how being a traveler awakens your mind to the reality that you are going somewhere. There is a destination, a purpose and reason for traveling, and it is to get somewhere.

This is a simple and perhaps obvious thought, but when I am at home, going to work, picking up my daughter from the bus stop, paying bills and doing the things I normally do, I do not have the mindset that I am going somewhere. I see myself as much more sedentary. A fixed point on the map. I don't really think of my life in terms of being *en route*.

I do not know of anyone who left home on a trip except that there was some reason or purpose behind it. [Note: Actually my brother Jon is on that kind of trip, but for him I think it is more of a philosophical statement which is itself a reason for traveling. Can a non-reason be a reason? I digress, but more on this and Jon later.]

Everyone has a reason for going: it may have been something as quirky as wanting to see the World's Largest Ball of String or as profound as visiting the grave of a parent.

The sense of mission, a goal, a target, is very strong when you travel. We have a place to go, something to see, a destination to reach. And I think the goal is different for everyone. For my father, that first trip was about going around the world. For my mother it was making it home alive and with the same number of boys with which she left.

Travelers are defined by their destinations. Otherwise it doesn't really make sense.

So it is totally understandable to me that Peter would want to remind these first century Christians, and us I think, to keep in mind their destination. They are tourists, strangers, but they are going somewhere. There is a point to all of this.

First he wants them to remember that they are going into a living hope. A weird destination, I concur; I don't think he means that little town in Arkansas.

He explains a little further what this hope is, or maybe I should say *where*. He writes that "In his great mercy [God] has given us new birth into a living hope through the resurrection of Jesus Christ from the dead." (1:3)

I don't think it is all that unusual to think of death as a destination. Maybe it's not exactly like going to Disney World or the beach, but I believe on some level we understand death as a place, a location at the end of the road. It is somewhere you go, or maybe more precisely, that comes to you. I have in my mind that creepy skeleton guy in a boat who comes to take you across the river Styx to your final resting place.

Regardless of your concept of death, Peter's point is that our destination is "into living hope;" it is somewhere beyond death, perhaps through death as if death were just a rest stop.

But because of the mercy of God (and who knows exactly how that works; you should check out Paul's discussion of this in Romans chapter 9), because of God's mercy we get to travel through, past, and beyond death into the hope of new life. That is a pretty good deal.

Sometimes you have to go through a crappy place to get to paradise; like you have to go through Philly to get to the Jersey Shore. I'm kidding, Philadelphia! You're beautiful, too. But you get my point.

The other really cool thing about this is the vehicle we get to ride in on this trip. We have all seen movies where some car or massive truck is running amok and smashing through fences and walls and buildings, flames and explosions going off all over the place.

One time when I was a kid living in Wyoming, a college student of my dad's came and got me in his big ol' Jeep after a huge snow storm. He took me around town and all we did was crash through giant snow drifts. It was incredible.

Peter writes that it is through the resurrection of Jesus that we get to our destination of a new birth and a living hope. Jesus and His resurrection is like a massive monster truck crashing through the walls and fences and snowdrifts of death, taking us to our new home. I'd call that truck something like Death Crusher. And of course his arch nemesis monster truck would be Grave Digger.

I think that is a pretty accurate description of what happened when Jesus died and then rose again three days later.

"Death has been swallowed up in victory.

"Where, O death, is your victory? Where, O death is your sting?" (1 Corinthians 15:54-55)

And that's not all. Not only are we going to a new hope, Peter goes on to explain that we are also headed into an *inheritance*. What?!

That is like going to your rich uncle's house. Or to a really nice resort. No one goes on vacation to places that suck. At least not normal people. People want to go to the exotic, the beautiful, the extravagant, the exclusive. That's why no one vacations in Laramie, Wyoming. It's just a normal place.

So not only are we headed to an inheritance, but one that can never perish, spoil or fade.

New Guinea is one of the most remote and exotic places on the planet. By remote I mean that in order to get to our village we had to drive nearly a whole day from the closest town of any size, over a treacherous, muddy, rutted out dirt track. After bouncing around for eight plus hours, more often than not having to pull the truck out of a mud bog somewhere along the way and inhaling several metric tons of diesel fumes, we would come to the end of the road. *From there* it was only another three- hour hike to our little bamboo house in the Kinona Valley. To me, that's remote; no roads, no hospitals, no nothing. It was beautiful. New Guinea is home to some of the most stunning flora and fauna anywhere. Deep rugged valleys and towering mountains; one minute you would find yourself walking through wind-swept, flowing seas of six-foot high kunai grass, the next you were deep in a humid rain forest surrounded by exquisite flowers and plants, huge vines hanging from the canopy high over head.

Fruit was everywhere. Mangoes, passion fruit, avocados, and bananas hung from every tree it seemed, and often as we hiked we would grab a quick snack to enjoy on the way.

The glorious songs of New Guinea's famed birds would echo in your head, and if you were lucky you might catch sight of the bird-of-paradise, a national treasure with long graceful feathers trailing behind it as it flies. Or perhaps you might see a cassowary, the ostrich's much smaller cousin, or small marsupials like the cuscus or sugar glider. This is not even to mention the wild boars, bats, hundreds of snakes and other reptile species, insects, fish and amphibians.

It is not at all unlike the Garden of Eden in my opinion. At least this is how I remember it when I was 11, our first time to the island.

I returned to New Guinea about 15 years later and things had changed significantly, if not entirely. The dirt road had been extended all the way into our little valley. One no longer had to press on through the tall grass or dense jungle, or ford the swiftly moving streams.

The road was dusty, trees pushed over, valleys filled in to make room for the winding ribbon of crushed rock and intermittent patches of blacktop. And with the increased traffic and economic development came more litter, more people, more aggression and violence.

It is hard not to think that things are slowly wearing down and that development, modernity, will eventually have its way with even the most unspoiled, rare places in New Guinea.

There are not many places in the world that have not or will not eventually perish, spoil and fade. Really there are none. I love that humanity is working hard to try to turn the tide of pollution and rampant waste, to be better stewards of the place God has given us to live, but I also believe that this is more than an uphill battle.

In the midst of this, I am so encouraged by Peter's reminder that we are going somewhere, we are travelers and tourists and we are headed into a place that will be perfect forever, a place that is "shielded by God's power until the coming of the salvation that is ready to be revealed in the last time." (1:5)

I am not one who likes to sit and home and never venture out into the unknown, but at the same time I like to know things are relatively safe.

When we first arrived in the Kinona Valley, many of the people from surrounding villages came out to greet us. That is an understatement actually; they had prepared more of an opening ceremonies.

As we walked down the final hill, through the long grass, warriors dressed in full battle regalia emerged. They wore headdresses adorned with colorful feathers and intricate grass weavings. Their faces were painted with the signs of their tribe, colored mud and berry juice. Each of them held a long bow and multiple, fierce and dangerous-looking arrows.

Joe started crying like a three-year old. He was four. Ridiculous. And I was taken back for a second, but it was hard to miss, even under all that face paint, those huge smiles and bright eyes that told the real story. They were thrilled we were there, that we had come to be part of their community and that those spears, those arrows were there to protect, not harm us.

Never once did I feel in any danger during our time in the Kinona Valley. I knew there was a shield around us; strong men who would protect and save us. Men and women who would see us through our stay and get us to the other side.

Kind of like Jesus in that big ol' monster truck.

JOIN THE CONVERSATION

Before you read the next chapter stop and read 1 Peter 1:6-12 and share what you think on Twitter at #Strangers&Aliens. I'd love to talk about what jumps out at you.

2 GLORIES THAT WOULD FOLLOW
1 Peter 1:6-12

Being a tourist or traveler in another country is difficult. Initially it is hard because you have no clue as to what is going on. You don't know the language (perhaps), you don't know where anything is, the money is weird. You are the object of all the annoyed and impatient sighs and eye rolling.

We lived in Budapest for about a year in the late '80s, and the first time we went to the local grocer was one of those kinds of experiences. Being released from decades of communist rule literally the week before we arrived, very few people had any experience with foreigners, much less my family.

I think my sweet little mother must have tried for 20 minutes to explain to the girl behind the deli counter that she wanted a kilometer of Swiss cheese, sliced. First of all, and I am no mathematician or an expert in the metric system, but I don't think you measure food in kilometers, and second, no matter how slowly you enunciate when you speak, it is still English and she has no idea what you are saying.

It was about a month before we had any cheese in our house. That level of frustration and effort going into something that normally should take about two seconds is not a lot of fun, which is why, I contend, we like tours and cruises where someone else handles all the details and logistics and we can just relax on the Aloha Deck with a margarita.

As time goes on, I think being a foreigner gets difficult for other reasons. Eventually you start to get how things work, where things are, how the bus system is laid out. You can get by with the basics. Live in a different country for an extended length of time, maybe six months or a year, and you start to feel a different kind weight. I don't know why it is, but on a deep, maybe subconscious level, you just realize this is not home.

At least that has been my experience.

I think part of it is that you know you will always be a stranger, an alien of sorts, but I think it is also that subconscious (or not) realization that *others* know you are not from these here parts. And then I think one of two things happens: one, you feel yourself becoming a burden and, two, you become a target.

Big, Grand Stories *(I Peter 1:6-7)*

When we lived in Hungary, my father was teaching at a university and so we met a number of students during our time there. This was literally right after the Cold War had ended in 1989, and because we were from the West, people thought we must be pretty interesting. Being from the United States our new friends had a lot of questions about our home, what America is like, etc. etc. It was tough to communicate because Hungarian is like no language I have ever heard and three years of middle school French did not help a lick. Fortunately we had Aron, the son of my father's Hungarian colleague, around a good bit of the time and he was a great translator who could bridge the gap.

My brother Tim and I would get invitations to go with our new friends to the university parties. Huge events with bands and DJs and movies and thousands of students from all over Budapest. It was always super crowded and loud; it made communicating difficult if you knew the language, and pretty much impossible if you needed someone to explain for you that you had never met Bruce Willis or Madonna because America is a very large place and you do not live in Beverly Hills.

Eventually, the effort it takes to have those kinds of conversations gets to be too much. I don't blame the students; it was hard on all of us. But you start to realize that there is this gap between you and the natives that is going to be really difficult to overcome, and in fact, you may never be able to do it, because if it isn't the language, it's how they see the world or understand history or view marriage or work or family or life or a million other things that separate us culturally.

I am not saying it's impossible, I'm just saying it is very difficult and there will always be something, even if it buried way down deep, that reminds us we are not from this place. And that gets heavy to carry.

But besides being a burden, I think that being a tourist can be difficult because, unfortunately, it makes you a target. We just stick out. That's the reality. We are the ones with the weird clothes (to them). We are the ones taking pictures of the pigeons and street vendors. We are the ones holding copious amounts of cash out in public, trying to figure out how much we need to use the public toilet. We are the ones irritated that we have to pay to use the public toilet.

Tourists are easy to spot. They have a certain way of walking: slow. And they never look down at the ground or where they are going, but always up, into the sky, as if they put all the good stuff on the tops of buildings.

I mean, who doesn't see a tourist and think, "Someone is going to rob that idiot."?

I have been robbed probably more times than I realize, but by far the most unnerving was a time my brother Tim and I traveled from Budapest in the VW bus we had shipped from Wyoming to the south of France. Nice, France to be exact. We were young and carefree and thought a trip to the Mediterranean coast would be a nice break from the grey Hungarian winter.

And I am sure it would have been, if we had made it that far.

We had been warned to be extra careful at hostels and to make sure to keep all our stuff with us and locked up, but of course we thought this was superfluous and unnecessary.

Normally, my brother Tim is a very prudent, attentive and astute traveler. Being the second son and having to live in the shadow of his awesome older brother, he distinguished himself with a sharp mind (*summa cum laude* in Computer Science in college), a good work ethic (ran in the national meet in the 3,000-meter steeplechase, a grueling race) and boyish charm (even at 40 he can hardly grow a beard). All these good qualities are why I fully blame him for what happened in the south of France.

After we left Budapest, we had a good 12-hour drive through the incredible mountains of northern Italy. We eschewed the main highways that cut directly through the mountains and spanned magnificent valleys and chose instead more local, winding routes up and over, down and through said mountains and valleys. The real reason was to avoid the tolls on the super highways, but the effect was that we got to enjoy some really quaint villages and hamlets. We also got pretty worn out pulling around all those tight corners in an old VW bus with no power steering.

We arrived just over the border to France late in the evening tired and hungry. All we wanted was a soft pillow and a little food. Confident the sun and beauty of the south of France would bring our spirits rejuvenation in the morning, we dove into our *Fodor's Europe* guidebook looking for a place cheap and close by where we could lay our weary heads.

I don't remember the name of the hostel or how we found the place in the pitch dark. I do remember we almost drove off a cliff, literally, having taken a wrong turn up a narrow mountain pass. Eventually we found the hostel and, plagued with a deadly combination of exhaustion, stupidity, laziness and optimism, we ignored all previous warnings and left most of our stuff in the car overnight.

I remember the next morning it was overcast and drizzling. As we walked to the van, which fortunately hadn't rolled off anywhere during the night, I recall a distinct premonition that something was not right.

And it wasn't.

When we got to the vehicle we realized someone had pulled the seal around the back window, removed the glass and taken all of our stuff. Our hearts sank. We had in there most of our clothes for the upcoming year. Now it looked like we would be walking around Budapest in acid wash jeans and some weird Air Soviet sneakers. At least we would blend in.

We filed a report with the Nice police, who were anything but. I cannot believe they had anything better to do that track down second-hand clothing for a couple of obviously naive American teenagers.

"Were the jeans Levi's? Ooh la la, this is a most disturbing case." Whatever, dude.

That was a long van ride home to the relative safety of the Communist East Bloc, cardboard window flapping in the breeze.

Trials and hardship, missed flights, lost luggage, frustration in communication, gross food, homesickness and getting lost; all this stuff is a part of being a traveler. It is inevitable, really, and never fun at the time. But here is the weird thing about all that stuff and the stories I have just shared: those are the things we talk about, those are the times on our trips that we remember and recount most often.

I don't know why this is, but hardship makes for such a better story than comfort and ease and everything going exactly as planned.

J.R.R. Tolkien wrote in *The Hobbit* that at one time the band of adventuring dwarves and a hobbit stopped in Rivendell, the home of the elves, where they got lots of rest, were well fed, and were protected from the all the harm and hardship of their trip. And Tolkien wrote that he didn't have much to really tell about that time, because it didn't make for a very good story. Ease and comfort are not exactly the makings of an adventure.

Peter writes to his travelers, "...now for a little while you may have had to suffer grief in all kinds of trials. These have come so that your faith--of greater worth than gold, which perishes even though refined by fire--may prove genuine and may result in praise, glory and honor when Jesus Christ is revealed." (1:7)

Being a tourist is difficult, but it is the trial, the pain, the trouble, that is of great worth. These stories are what we remember and recount. These stories are what amount to our praise, glory and honor when we finally get home. No one wants to hear about how you sat by the pool and shoveled ice cream and lobster tail into your face all day. Everyone wants to hear about how you punched a pickpocket on a bus in Mexico City (as did my father, but more on this later).

I think that when we are finally home, when we are reunited with Christ, when we are all sitting around after dinner, the fire is going and we are sipping on the best coffee ever, we will start to tell stories. And they will be stories of those who went through the fire, went through some serious trials like the countless people who died for their faith, those who were persecuted because they wanted to live a life that honored God, those who faced sickness and loss of loved ones and did not waver in their faith.

Big, grand stories.

And I think we will tell stories of those quiet moments when some of us struggled and wrestled with doing the right thing, and we overcame. I think there will be loud cheers for those tales of triumph in overcoming, praise and glory and honor.

Searched Intently *(1 Peter 1:8-12)*

My dad is a people person. He can talk to absolutely anyone about anything. The other night he and my mother and I were out to dinner with some friends and he was at the end of the table deeply engaged in conversation with my good friend, Mark. Mark is about 6' 2", 240. He played football at Grove City College about ten years ago.

Well, my dad had been chewing on Mark's ear for most of the night, so finally I asked Lauren, Mark's wife, what in the world they were talking about.

"The Denison women's basketball team played Grove City last week."

My dad went to Denison in the late '50s and lives part of the year about 20 steps from campus. He goes to almost every athletic event at the school. I am sure he wanted to know Mark's opinion on the Lady Grovers (that's really what they call people who go to GCC) and the outlook for the upcoming season. Mark didn't even know Grove City had a women's basketball team, much less the free throw percentage of the second string power forward.

My father has always had this innate curiosity that has driven him to people. He wants to know what they think, what they've seen. He wants to know what's out there.

Many, many times while traveling, my dad will stop a complete stranger on the street and 30 minutes later come back to the rest of us and tell us how he found out we have to go to such-and-such a place because so-and-so, whom he just met, said how great it was. And I have to give him some credit--he has found out about some pretty cool stuff that way. I am pretty sure that is how we ended up on the Trans Siberian Express, a train that runs from Moscow to Beijing in a mere nine days. Incredible.

I am not so much wired this way. I think it's because I'm afraid that asking questions, being curious, may tip people off that I'm not as bright or experienced or knowledgeable as I would like for people to think that I am. It takes a certain amount of humility and courage to be curious. In that way I wish I were more like my dad.

For some reason, Peter includes a little section that I think is meant to give his readers a broader perspective on what is going on with them. I think he wants them to know that this is pretty big, these things he is telling them. I think it bears quoting what Peter says at length:

"Concerning this salvation, the prophets, who spoke of the grace that was to come to you, searched intently and with the greatest care, trying to find out the time and circumstances to which the Spirit of Christ in them was pointing when he predicted the sufferings of Christ and the glories that would follow. It was revealed to them that they were not serving themselves but you, when they spoke of the things that have now been told you by those who preached the gospel to you by the Holy Spirit sent from heaven. Even angels long to look into these things." (1:10-12)

Two things jump out at me in the paragraph. First, that the prophets searched intently and with great care to learn about and figure out the whole suffering and subsequent glory of Christ. This was, of course, in reference to his death on the cross and subsequent resurrection and ascension into heaven. I mean they were intrigued by that, this caught their attention, in fact so much so that they were intensely and carefully searching to figure out what in the world this was all about.

The second thing about this really blows my mind for some reason. It kind of makes me even wonder about Peter's credibility to be honest. He writes that even the angels are curious about this.

I have no idea how he knows this other than the Holy Spirit told him, "Hey Peter, all the angels up here are dying to look into this whole thing with Jesus and his suffering and then the glories that are going to come after it. They are really pumped."

Curiosity, man. People are drawn into those kinds of stories. Think about it: would you rather watch a movie about some rich guy laying in bed all day eating bon-bons while servants wait on him or the guy who fails and gets up and falls down and gets up and finally overcomes and wins? That's why those ridiculous Rocky movies made a zillion dollars. He was telling the story of Jesus. And it is a *really* good story. The Jesus one; I thought Rocky lost a little momentum after about movie eight or nine.

Curiosity, the hope of a great story, is what motivates the traveler to press on, to get up and move. To take risks and explore new worlds, to find new ways of doing things, new ways of looking at the world.

I am pretty sure that most of the time I am completely oblivious to the true story I am currently living. I have convinced myself that my story goes something like this: I wake up, brush my teeth, go to work, work, go home, brush my teeth, go to bed. Wash, rinse, repeat. The French existentialists call this *métro, boulot, dodo*, and it is what drives people insane. At least people who think about it very deeply.

Most of us, I believe, are convinced, deep down, that we live the most boring lives in the world. It is what prompted Thoreau to write, "The mass of men lead lives of quiet desperation."

Peter's point is this, I think: you should be insanely curious and fascinated by this life of suffering, this life of a stranger, this life of Jesus; it is so interesting even the prophets and angels are enthralled by it.

No one likes a boring story. No one wants a life that is dull and mundane. I think Peter is encouraging us to look into the life of Christ, the kind of life he lived and wants us to live, too. A life that is different, strange, that is full of trials and difficulties, hope and reward, suspense and intrigue. I think this is what he wants for us. And I want to live a life where things fascinate me.

This is the life of the traveler, often beset with trouble, wrong turns, missed flights and sometimes opposition and running up against cranky border guards, lost luggage, bad directions. But it is full of glory, unimagined sights and smells and sounds and adventures for those who are willing to push out from the shore, to set off into the unknown.

JOIN THE CONVERSATION

Before you read the next chapter stop and read 1 Peter 1:13-2:3 and share what you think on Twitter at #Strangers&Aliens. I'd love to talk about what jumps out at you.

3 THE SEPARATED LIFE
1 Peter 1:13-2:3

I think I am like most people in that I spend more energy and emotion than I should trying not to be the weirdo. Oh sure, I like to think that I am unique and special and all that, but deep down the reality is I don't want to be the oddball, the dummy wearing Bugle Boy jeans when everyone else is wearing Levi's. I am pretty sure this actually happened in the eighth grade at one point.

There is something kind of innate within us that wants to be part of the herd, to not get out there too far on our own. We like to be around what is familiar, what is like us. We feel safe there, probably like a zebra–if he wanders too far from the herd those crazy stripes really stick out like some bizarre Girl Scout cookie. Stay in the herd and you're safe.

Cain was the first traveler. The first tourist, sort of. He was told by God to leave the place where he had grown up (and murdered his brother by the way) and go wander the land. He really didn't like that idea--too vulnerable, too out there, even though God said He would protect him. So Cain basically said, "Thanks anyway" and headed for the city. Figured he would settle down, get married, have some kids, build a wall, live the life of the masses.

Nothing makes you feel more different and disconnected than when you are a tourist in another country. Being a traveler enunciates differences: an understanding that you have a different way of seeing the world. Want to feel strange? Strap on a fanny pack, some long socks and sandals and head overseas. (Or stay where you are and do that. Bad example.)

Perhaps the most acute experience I have had with this was a time my brother and I were driving through some German town, a city really, in our old VW bus. If you know my family and our history with the automobile, you will not be surprised to learn that not only did we now have a cardboard window thanks to our escapades in Nice, but this particular vehicle could only be started by pushing it manually. (This was best accomplished rolling down a hill if you were lucky and/or blessed with enough foresight to park on a hill or incline.)

To get the thing started, you had to get some momentum built up. And usually that meant a profound amount of grunting, sweating, and sometimes cursing until you reached terminal velocity, the point at which the clutch could be released, and in turn might, after a series of violent mechanical epileptic convulsions, start the engine.

The trick with driving this kind of vehicle is to not stall. Ever. Because if you do, someone is going to have to get out and push, and they will no doubt be cussing you under their breath the whole time.

And I don't know how many of you have been to Germany, but Germany is where they make a lot of cars. A lot of nice cars. Our Volkswagen in fact was a German car, but that was a different era, and if you think driving a VW van in Germany would help us to blend in, well, you would be wrong. Very wrong. No, Germans drive new cars, expensive cars: Mercedes-Benz, Audi, BMW. They drive fast, with precision and, I'm just guessing here, but I don't think any of them had to drift start to get to work in the morning.

Anyway, Tim and I were in one of these German towns, Audis flying past us like we were a couple of old ladies on our way to bingo. Suddenly we hit a red light, which normally we would run without conscience, but we had to stop because there was a car in front of us. When you have to push to start your car you don't stop for much, so red lights, especially in crowded cities, were viewed mostly as a "good idea," but not always "necessary."

In any case, any time we had to stop it always created a bit of tension with our starter situation the way it was. But we were cool. Just a Volkswagen parked at a red light; nothing strange or out of the ordinary here.

Now I am not totally sure who was driving at this point, but since I'm writing this book, it was definitely Tim. Suffice it to say that once the light turned green, the restart did not go so well. A little light on the gas, a little quick on the clutch. A violent hiccup and cloud of smoke and we were dead in the water. Stalled.

The rest is really a blur. Traffic begins to move, Germans speaking in tongues cursing the idiots holding up progress ahead. Cars start whizzing past us. The tension begins to mount.

Fortunately this wasn't the first time this had happened. And so one of us needed to be the hero (and let's not get hung up on who did what or when), so one of us reacted with catlike reflexes, threw open the side door of the van like a SWAT team commando, and with sudden, Herculean effort (like when a father is able to lift an airplane off his trapped daughter's leg), the car began to roll. It moved slowly at first, confused/angry/annoyed Germans looking at us out their windows as they sped by, slowly gnawing their morning strudel.

We picked up speed, massive muscles and sinews straining against what had to be the several tons of rusted metal and bolts and baling wire and wood paneling we called a car.

Finally we reached adequate speed, the clutch popped, the motor coughed, sputtered, caught for a second, belched an enormous mushroom cloud of black smoke, and by some miracle finally turned and started. Our hero jumped in, collapsed on the floor pulling in deep breaths of precious oxygen, and off we sped to our next adventure at approximately 25 miles per hour. The humiliation, soon enough, would be far behind.

It is never fun being the weirdo, being different. And yet there is something really cool about it, too. That is one of my favorite stories and one of my best memories with my brother. I laugh every time I think of it. In retrospect, I am glad we had that old bus. In retrospect.

Peter reminds us that in our calling as strangers, tourists and travelers in this life, we are different, we are separated from those around us. Like Cain, we are simply travelers here, temporary inhabitants, and as such, that kind of puts us on the outside of things.

Peter uses the word "holy," which in spite of whatever theological baggage that word may carry for you simply means "set apart." It means that we are to see ourselves, understand and experience the world, from a position of separateness. And at times that feels like driving a 1973 VW bus when everyone else is in a Mercedes Benz.

Being Holy *(1 Peter 1:13-16)*

I think when Peter encourages these people to be holy, what he is really asking them to remember is that they are different, they are strangers, and because of this there should be a certain distance between them, how they see the world and how they act in the world. "Do not conform to the evil desires you had" literally means do not connect with them. Remain separate, unaffected.

It is not easy to be unaffected by the trends and tides of opinion that surround us, to be separate in the sense Peter is meaning here. For some reason it is much more natural for us to go along with the crowd, to blend in and just do what everyone else is doing.

I have only ever once been in a full-out food fight. It was in ninth grade at Laramie Junior High School. The buzz had been building all day that this was going to go down at lunch; kids were passing notes in chemistry, flashing signs at each other in the hallway. The air was thick with anticipation. Even the teachers seemed on edge, their eyes narrowed, assessing each student carefully trying to confirm the rumors, but also to let us know such insolence would be handled with swift justice and without discrimination for any who dared participate.

The lunchroom was uncharacteristically quiet that day--just the clatter of an occasional fork against a plastic tray, the scraping of a chair on the linoleum floor. An eagle screamed from some distant corner. Students whispered under their breath, a low constant buzz like a hoard of cicadas. You could hear them, you knew they were lying in wait, you just didn't know exactly what was going to happen.

But there was something else just a little off. Something that did not seem quite normal. The room was full, only a few empty chairs at a table here and there. The teachers were all there, pacing the floor, going between tables and along the perimeter of the cafeteria like anxious prison guards. But there was something else.

And then I saw it.

Our lunchroom had a main seating area with probably 25-30 tables of 8-10 seats each, which is where most of the kids sat. But there was also a raised platform on the far wall that was used as a stage at different times during the year. Up there were probably another 7-8 tables full of hyped-up pre-teens all sitting on one side of their table. The side *facing* the main floor, ensuring they all had a good view of the room.

In the larger, lower section, every kid was on the side of their table facing the platform. It was obvious; no one wanted their back turned when all hell broke loose. I have never read *The Art of War*, but I am pretty sure it states that the attack always comes from the high ground.

We had baloney subs that day, with American cheese, mustard, mayo, lettuce and tomato on a hoagie roll. Side of green beans and applesauce. White milk and a snickerdoodle.

I slid into my seat, one of the last to get lunch that day, and waited. We all waited.

Two hundred and fifty junior highers silent as a church on Monday would make anyone nervous. That many kids have way too much energy to stay bottled up for very long. It is like blowing up a balloon; you keep blowing and blowing in spite of the tension you know is building. And you know, at some point, it is going to explode. You just don't know exactly when.

There is still some debate as to who sent the first sub flying, but I distinctly remember Jay Francesco (on the stage) standing up in the middle of the silence and whipping a sub at Doug Kramer (main level). I am not sure he yelled, "Food fight!" but I like to think he did.

The effect of this single act was as if you had just made that final turn on a jack-in-the-box. Kablooey. The sky was filled with food. Baloney, cheese and snickerdoodles rained down like fire and brimstone on Gomorrah. Innocent little seventh graders, hair tied up in braids and who just last period were dotting their i's with hearts in Home Ec, were transformed in an instant into guerrilla warriors, ambushing ninth grade football players with applesauce and green beans.

Tables were flipped up on end, students diving for cover as if their very lives depended on it. Teachers were running about, impervious to the hailstorm of food, grabbing anyone they saw participating. Some had four or five students under an arm.

It was an all-out war.

Now I tell you all that to set the context for what was going on in my mind. I entered the lunchroom that day pretty much knowing all this was going to happen, although the fact that it actually went down did catch me (and probably everyone else) off guard a little. And to be honest, I did not plan to throw any food. I wasn't a goody two-shoes or anything, but I did know that a food fight was probably not a good idea and I should probably stay out of it.

I don't know what happened really, what came over me. I remember being behind an overturned table, food flying over my head, the floor littered with culinary carnage. A single cookie rolled from around the corner of the table and came to rest near my hand.

How I got to this point I do not know, but I do remember thinking, "I don't want to be the only one in the school who won't have a story to tell after this is all done." No one was in my ear, no one was telling me to throw it, that I was a nerd or anything like that. This was all happening in my *head*. It was mental. Am I going to be like everyone else or not? Simple question.

Peter writes, "Therefore, prepare your minds for action; be self-controlled.... Be holy [different] in all you do." (1:13, 15, brackets mine)

I threw the cookie.

I threw the cookie because in my mind I was not prepared for the situation; I had not mentally gotten myself to the place where I knew what I was going to do. I think that is a lot what self-control is about. It is about pre-planning, knowing going in what lines you will not cross so that when those boundaries are tested, in the heat of battle, you already know the answer, what you are or are not going to do.

I was caught unprepared.

I threw the cookie because everyone else was doing it and I didn't want to be different. It's a lame reason, but that's the truth of it. And even though I cannot condone food fights, I have a certain level of respect for Jay Francesco. He stood up in the middle of that cafeteria when no one else would and he flung that baloney sandwich without fear or consideration of what anyone thought.

There is something kind of holy about that. In a distorted, juvenile way, sure. But holy nonetheless.

Not that being different is the goal, but some of the most intriguing, captivating people I know are those who seem totally unaffected by the opinions and trends of the crowd around them. They are kind, nice, polite, sociable, but totally unaffected by what others think. They are just going to do what God says is right. In my mind, that is holiness. And I like it.

I left the lunchroom that day and headed back to my locker to get my books for sixth period history. A lone piece of lunch meat stuck to the cinder block wall slowly started to peel and then suddenly fell to the ground.

From This Empty Way of Life *(1 Peter 1:17-21)*

Every once in awhile I will have an out-of-body experience. I know that sounds a bit odd to say because you probably think I am a pretty normal guy and I would like to believe that I am.

What I mean by an "out-of-body" experience is that sometimes I will get in the frame of mind where I kind of see myself from a third person perspective. Somehow, mentally, I kind of detach from my physical body and am able to look at myself from an outside perspective. It is kind of like the Gestalt switch-thing where you look at that picture and can see the young woman and then bam! you see an old woman. Only I am not an old woman, I just see myself from a distance.

Kind of weird, I know.

Many times this will take place in front of a mirror in the bathroom, maybe at home or in a restaurant. I will look at my reflection and for some reason I view myself as not myself but as someone else named Trey. He has short brown hair, a long thin nose and a mole on his cheek. He needs to shave and maybe should change out of that black quarter-zip fleece at least once this week.

It is an odd thing to view oneself from that perspective, from the outside. It always freaks me out a bit to be honest because I wonder if this is what others see, if this is the Trey they are familiar with. For some reason, from that vantage point I feel a lot less significant, like I have less substance. The things I care about seem trivial, my life goals seems futile and childish. I guess when I look at myself from the outside I feel irrelevant, tertiary, unimportant. There is something empty there.

I know it is me, there in the mirror, but I also on some level wonder if it really is. I sense this estrangement from myself, a very distinct, very real separation. Like I know I am looking at myself, but at the same time I am not sure I really am.

Sometimes I get the feeling there is nothing I can do to escape who I am, this shell of a body that I have been given. I have this face, these arms and legs and that is all there is to it, but at the same time, that is not really who I am, but what I am is something inside, trapped in the flesh and bone that I see in the mirror.

It is kind of like magnets held only a few millimeters apart; I can still feel the attraction, the connectedness between physical and soulful Trey, but we are separate for a moment. Then, snap--we merge back together, trapped again.

A friend of mine has a quote on her Facebook profile from C.S. Lewis. "You don't have a soul, you are a soul. You have a body." I think this is so profound and on a very real level describes what is going with me in my out-of-body experiences; I think I am sensing the distinction between my soul and my body and I wonder if that is the way it will always be.

Without going all Grandpa on you, let me just say that the body tends to wear down as you get older. I know, I never thought it would happen either. When I was 18 my body looked and responded much differently than now, on the other side of 40. To be honest I am really hoping that I can trade this body in for something a little more stylish and with a little more horsepower. But it is hard not to think this is what we are stuck with, this is what we will have to wear around for the duration. Science is doing its best to maintain and reshape what we have, but they have yet to extract us, our soul, from this body and put it into a new one.

One of the things I did not expect when we moved to New Guinea was our almost daily struggle and battle with mud. We have mud in America of course, but nothing like there. Here we have sidewalks and roads and drainage systems for rainwater. In New Guinea there are dirt paths, and when it rains, which happens literally every day, those paths become quagmires, knee-deep bogs from which it can be difficult if not impossible to escape.

I think we were on our way to another village, maybe Kasokana or Ekoti, when my father got stuck in one such mud hole. I think the ground looked a little more stable than it actually was, otherwise I do not think he would have tried to cross. Of course, sometimes you just underestimate the power of mud and its absolute ability to incapacitate you. The thing is with mud, it is easy to step in, but when you try to extract your foot, the mixture of water and dirt creates a powerful vacuum and it becomes nearly impossible to get out.

A couple of wrong steps and it had a hold of my father. First one leg and then the other. Up to his knees.

To say my dad is dramatic is a bit of an understatement. If he stubs his toe on a chair, the resulting yell would lead you to believe it had actually been chopped off. Dogs hide, small children start to cry, a flock of birds is startled from a neighboring tree.

I am sure it was not funny to him, but to the rest of us not stuck, it was pretty hilarious. He looked like some kind of underwater seaweed plant, totally immobile from the waist down, but waist up, arms flailing violently as if by sheer will and volume of grunts and yells he could fling himself to safety.

You may have heard this about quicksand, but the same is true of mud--the harder you try, the more you become stuck. Basically you have to give up if you are ever going to get out. And you are going to need help from someone not stuck.

I think the notion of being rescued is offensive to us for some reason. Perhaps it is because of our pioneering, independent American spirit. Manifest destiny, first ones on the moon, defenders of freedom. We really do not like the idea that we might need someone, might need some help sometimes. We hate to have to ask for help. Just ask the average man how much he likes to stop and ask for directions. My brother Tim, the human map as I mentioned earlier, just bought a new car and refused to get one with built-in GPS. He told me it was an offense to his geographical sensibilities.

Peter writes, "...live your lives as strangers here in reverent fear. For you know it was not with perishable things such as silver and gold that you were redeemed from the empty way of life handed down to you from your forefathers, but with the precious blood of Christ, a lamb without blemish or defect...so your faith and hope are in God." (1:17-21)

I think it takes a certain amount of humility, fear, to admit we need to be rescued. I can probably count on one hand the number of times I cried out for help or asked someone to give me a hand, especially when I have been a traveler. I never wanted to seem like a tourist, like I don't know where I'm going or can't figure something out. I have no doubt I should have asked many more times in my life. I probably would have experienced a much richer life if I had.

The other thing that strikes me about Peter's statement here is the comparison he makes between "perishable" silver and gold and the "precious" blood of Christ. He asserts that we were rescued (from an empty way of life, mind you), not with something else that is worthless or will also pass away, but rather with something wholly different, something *other*, something precious: the blood of Christ.

I am really no theologian, that much should be obvious by now, and I really don't get all the mechanics, or the "how" of this kind of spiritual rescue, but it seems to me what Peter is saying is that in order to be rescued from the current world in which we find ourselves, it had to be something *from the outside* that came in and did the rescuing. It couldn't be gold and silver because that kind of stuff is stuck in the mud with us. It is mired in the same system and world that we are.

No, it had to be something from another world. To mix metaphors a bit, kidnapped people do not ransom themselves. They are rescued by people on the outside.

It would be a mistake, I believe, in Peter's opinion, for us to think that our life as travelers, as strangers in the world, is based on some corruptible financial economic system: silver and gold. To try to buy or earn holiness with something from within the same system from which we are trying to extract ourselves would be like trying to pull ourselves out of quicksand with a rope attached to the quicksand. Kind of futile.

I think this is the key point of the Gospel: to separate us from this empty way of life, to make us holy, God had to be Himself separate. "You were redeemed...with the precious blood of Christ, a lamb without blemish or defect." (1:18-19)

It is a good feeling to be set free. We left my dad in the mud for a little longer than we had to, but eventually someone handed him a branch or a rope or something and got him out of that mud hole. It is a good feeling to finally be able to move about, to not be tied down with the weight of life.

People often talk about the freedom of the open road and I think there is really something to that. When we escape our normal routine we experience a new kind of liberty. We do not have the same burdens, life is full of possibility, we can even, in a sense, become whatever we want to be. We are free to understand ourselves in a new way, a self that is not constrained to the cultural and social expectations that get piled on to our personalities from a very young age.

We are free. Freed by the precious blood of Christ to a new and better life. As Peter penned, "He (Jesus) was chosen before the creation of the world, but was revealed in these last times for your sake. Through him you believe in God, who raised him from the dead, and so your faith and hope are in God." (1:20-21)

I don't always get it. I don't always get how Jesus' blood frees me today, but I believe it and it gives me hope. It gives me hope that there is something beyond this shell, this peculiar body I seem, at times, attached to yet separate from. I have hope that I am moving on, being freed to something entirely new.

Now That You Have Tasted *(1 Peter1:22-2:3)*

Kids can be pretty funny, but they are not logical at all. Two of my closest friends, Mark and Lauren, have three young boys, Jack, Luke and George, and they say and do some of the funniest things ever.

Right now Luke is three and in the potty training process. It has been a long haul for him. The poor kid fell asleep on the toilet the other day. He is pretty stubborn. Lauren told me that a few days ago he was up in the attic playing with his brother when all of a sudden he came running into the kitchen.

"Mom, a dog pooped in the attic!"

"What?!" said Lauren. She admitted later that she was thinking at that moment, "How did a dog get into the house?!"

"Yes, a dog," he replied very matter-of-factly. "He pooped in the attic."

"But Luke, we don't have a dog." At this, little Luke got a bit introspective, which he is apt to do when pondering something. He obviously had not thought this through all the way. And mom is a pretty tough interrogator. He turned his head slightly sideways, scratched his chin with his little finger, honestly perplexed.

"Maybe it was a wolf, Mommy." (Why he thought it might have been a wolf I have no idea, except that to him wolves probably seem pretty devious and sinister and the creature most likely to both sneak into their house and have the courage to poop in the attic.)

"There was no wolf in the attic, Moose." (This is Luke's nickname, mainly because "Bull- In-A-China-Shop" takes too long to yell.)

I think at this point he probably was really confused and truly wondering what creature, what animal would have the audacity to desecrate the family living quarters in such a gross, base manner?

"Maybe it was Baby George." Wrong again.

"George is wearing a diaper. Was it you, Luke? Did you poop in the attic?"

Luke paused slightly, then remembering that his mom had taken off his diaper--the potty training equivalent of throwing your kid in the pool to teach him to swim--a little grin came over his face as if he was just now figuring it out with his mother.

"Yeah, Mommy, I pooped in the attic."

Like I said, funny, but not all that logical. I think if Luke had just studied the facts in a more reasonable and systematic manner he would have come to the proper conclusion on his own. But he is a kid and they are just not thinkers.

I think every parent has had this conversation with their kid at dinner one time or another:

Parent: "Eat your _____, you'll like it."

Kid: "No, I don't like it."

Parent: "How do you know? You've never even tried it before!"

Kid: "I don't like it."

And that is pretty much the end of the discussion. You will be unable to convince or reason with your child that what is on their plate is not only good for them, but it tastes good, too. I had that debate with my daughter about cucumbers. She wouldn't eat them no matter what I did to try to convince her otherwise.

Now she loves them. She'll eat a whole cucumber by herself. I am not sure what happened, but I think she saw how much her cousin Andy likes them. He is about her age and I think you just tend to trust people your own age for some reason.

Most people have this inherent distrust of new things. We are wary of new people, new places, new things. And I think this apprehension only grows with age. We probably get tired of being lied to, cheated, disappointed. We would much rather just stick with what we know, what is familiar and consistent.

This is the reason McDonald's is so successful. They realized a long time ago that people want to know what they are getting. You can go into a McDonald's in Budapest or anywhere in the world and your Big Mac is going to taste just like the one in your hometown.

Ask for a burger from a street vendor in New Guinea and you may get a piece of undercooked beef, topped with juicy red beets, all on a soggy pink bun. But that is a story for another time.

Traveling is a risk. You depend a lot on the advice of other people, whether it is by word-of-mouth or a travel guide or a show on television. When you step out and try something new, you are taking someone's word for it.

I suppose that is a big part of faith; believing that God has our good in mind and that the new things He asks us to try or do are for our benefit and not for our harm or His own sadistic amusement. I am pretty sure I do not ask my daughter to eat her broccoli because I enjoy watching her almost gag with each bite. I do it because I know it is good for her and because eventually she will come to see that broccoli actually tastes pretty good.

And it is part of life, it is a part of growing up. You have to get out there, try new things. It is very easy to get locked into one way of thinking, one way of living life. And I am pretty sure that God wants to give us a new life, a new way of being in the world.

Peter makes a few interesting points to his readers:

First, you can trust God because God's Word does not fade, it is living and enduring. He quotes Isaiah:

"All men are like grass,
    and all their glory is like the flowers of the field;
the grass withers and the flowers fall,
    but the word of the Lord endures forever." (40:6-8)

I think what he is getting at here is that God is someone you can trust. His Word is eternal, it will not disintegrate, it is true. And there is something to be said about that. We live in a world where we are probably very wise to not trust what most people say. We get lied to every day, by just about everyone. I think our skepticism is well earned.

But let's not throw God out with the bathwater. Maybe people claiming to speak for God have lied to you, deceived you, but God hasn't. He has and will always tell you the truth.

And I know that whole proposition begs the question, well, what is God saying? And there are a million ways to read the Bible and a million interpretations and ways to understand it. And depending on who you talk to, you get different instructions. And I am just not smart enough to figure it all out on my own.

These are all fair and important questions. Too much to cover right now, but let me just say this: I think God has always been able to communicate with those who have the heart to hear. Jesus' followers were uneducated men, so I don't believe you have to have a seminary degree to get what God is trying to tell you. I think you just have to be humble and open enough to listen and to trust that what Jesus said is true when He told His disciples when He was about to leave, "All this I have spoken while still with you. But the Counselor, the Holy Spirit, whom the Father will send in my name, will teach you all things and will remind you of everything I have said to you." (John 14:25-26)

Peter is also telling us that what we have tasted of God is good, so we should keep on eating. God is leading us, as travelers, as tourists, to a new way of living, and we should not be afraid to take a big ol' bite.

"Like newborn babies, crave pure spiritual milk, so that by it you may grow up in your salvation, now that you have tasted that the Lord is good."

(2:2-3)

I don't know a lot about babies, but I do know that they love their milk. They can be downright vicious about it. I have been around some nursing mothers and those kids can sound like a linebacker slurpin' on a Slurpee. They can't get enough. And they seem to know instinctively that what their mother is giving them is good.

Peter is telling us that God wants us to taste a new kind of life. One with which we are very unfamiliar I think, but one that is good and nourishing.

"Therefore, rid yourselves of all malice and deceit, hypocrisy, envy, and slander of every kind." (2:1)

None of us would even begin to say that we would want to live on a steady diet of malice or slander or hypocrisy. But the thing is, I am not sure that is true. In fact, I think we are more comfortable with that plate than the opposite: love, truth, authenticity, generosity and praise.

The difference between the two lists comes down to this, in my opinion:

In the former, we are concerned about ourselves. Malice is the aggressive assertion of our own will over that of someone else. Deceit is always employed in order to gain an advantage over another. Hypocrisy covers our true self and makes us look better than we really are. Envy looks at what we don't have and others do (and probably fuels malice and deceit to boot). Slander tears down others to make ourselves higher.

In the latter list, we put others first: love means dying to ourselves and considering others more important than ourselves. Truth means answering honestly even when it is to our own disadvantage. Authenticity means revealing our hidden selves, especially our failings, for all to see. Generosity means giving, even when we have little for ourselves. Praise means speaking highly of others and celebrating their victories rather than our own.

Peter is suggesting we shift from a life that is focused on ourselves to one that is focused on others. To a way of being that is about serving and dying for others rather than being served and getting for ourselves. Take a bite and see if you like it.

We have tasted this and have seen that God is good because this is how God is, this is what happened on the cross when Jesus forgot about Himself and what was owed Him and He died for us. And there is something about when someone loves you in that way that just makes you realize that's a good way to live, that's the kind of person we should want to be.

We probably tend to romanticize what Jesus did. We gloss over the brutality of the beatings, the pain and humiliation of hanging naked, nailed to a post, in front of hundreds if not thousands of people. We don't really get or want to think about the agony of gasping and straining for each breath until finally there was no strength left.

Dying to ourselves for others is no easy thing. But it is pure, spiritual milk--good and good for us.

JOIN THE CONVERSATION

Before you read the next chapter stop and read 1 Peter 2:4-12 and share what you think on Twitter at #Strangers&Aliens. I'd love to talk about what jumps out at you.

4 INTO A SPIRITUAL HOUSE
1 Peter 2:4-12

My dad had a saying he would use a lot when the four of us boys were growing up. More of a declaration than a saying, I suppose. It would unfold like this: someone would do or propose something that didn't quite sit right with him. Suddenly he would retort, "Not in my house!" Or the derivative, "As long as I am paying the mortgage, then you will do it how I say we do…and do it!" The last little part always coming after some incoherent mumblings under his breath about how things were different in his day and kids these days, that kind of thing.

Every home and family is unique in its own way. We all have our little idiosyncrasies and ways of doing things that, to the outsider, probably seem odd. Our family was no different.

Anytime a friend came over to spend the night on a Saturday, they had to go to church with us the next morning, which explains why I didn't have any friends on the weekends.

For our annual Thanksgiving Day football game we used to shovel our front lawn, piling feet of snow on the sidewalks. Sorry, pedestrians.

When we went on trips we never got a enough beds at the hotel for everyone to sleep on. "We're not here to sleep," my father would say. This practice led to some pretty awkward moments looking back, including one time I brought a girlfriend to my cousin's wedding; she met my parents for the first time and a couple hours later ended up having to sleep with my mother and sister-in-law in a double bed. It was either that or the floor next to the bathroom. We had about eight of us in the room for two nights.

Unfortunately I thought this was all perfectly normal, until I went to college and got to talk to people from the outside whose families believe it to be a basic human right for everyone to get to sleep on a mattress on vacation. I was shocked to find out we were the only family on the planet not to do that. I felt a little like I had just escaped from the Dunham Family Compound or something.

But my dad, maybe my mom, but I know definitely my dad did not really care what other people thought. He was doing things the way he saw best. I think it is one of his greatest strengths. He was building his house, his boys, according to a different set of values, a different way of looking at the world.

My parents shopped at garage sales because they wanted to be able to take their boys to see the world. We never had a new car or new furniture all the time I was growing up. I am not sure my mother ever bought a new item of clothing. She thought Goodwill was just fine for her. To be honest this irritated my dad who always tried to buy her fancy clothes. She would just respond, "Honestly, Paul!"

In spite of our eccentricities (and I think every family has them) our house was a great place to be. There was a lot of love there; I know this because I felt it, but I also saw how our friends wanted to be there. I don't remember too many meals when we didn't have an extra guest or two. I am proud of how my parents built our house.

I think it is interesting that Peter uses the metaphor of a house to describe what God is doing with His people. A house is where a family lives, where meals are shared, where people laugh and cry together. A house is a roof under which values are learned and passed down, and young lives are built into something. Hopefully something good, but maybe sometimes less than that.

I don't think anyone can appreciate how hard it is to be a parent until you have your own kid. And I think it is hard enough to just make sure they have pants on everyday when they head out the door, much less to try to teach them a set of values or how to do the right thing. Building a house in that sense is not easy.

Peter writes that God is building us into a spiritual house, a living house. This house, though, is built out of people, like a family, and put together in a different way, but one that is acceptable to Him. He is building this house, this family, in line with His values and His way of doing things.

Peter continues that Jesus Christ is the foundation, the chief cornerstone for this house. Like my father, in this house, we do it His way. And I think for Peter this means just one thing: we suffer, we serve, we lay down our lives for others. In this house, we are all about "offering spiritual sacrifices acceptable to God through Jesus Christ." (2:5)

This is a different kind of house that God is building. That much should be evident because it is being built on Jesus and He is so different, and sees people and the world from such a unique perspective. It makes sense that any house God would build would be totally different from anything anyone has ever seen before.

While I don't want to be a total oddball, I like being a little different. I like the contrary. I'm drawn to it for some reason. I used to work at a church where the norm was to tuck your shirt in, especially when teaching on Sunday mornings, so I would always leave mine out. When that became normal I started tucking mine back in.

I don't think I am a trendsetter or anything, and there are tons of days I just want to go with the flow. Sometimes though, I just can't help but buck the norm.

Maybe that is what is so attractive about Jesus. When people heard Him teach they said things like, "We have never heard someone teach like this." He astonished them with what He was saying. No one had seen the kind miracles He was performing: the lame could walk, the blind could see, the dead came back to life. This is not normal stuff. People came from everywhere to see what this new guy was doing. They were amazed and intrigued, and I think many people started to fall in love with Him.

But not everyone likes change, not everyone likes for the *status quo* to be challenged.

I keep a very neat refrigerator. I mean *very* neat. Everything has a very specific place. For example, right now I can tell you, without looking, that milk, coffee beans and creamer are on the second shelf of the door. Right above that are the most used condiments: strawberry jam, mayo, honey mustard and salsa. I can also tell you that yogurt, sour cream and cottage cheese are in one row on the top shelf and tubes of ready-to-make biscuits, croissants and cinnamon rolls in the next.

There is a fruit drawer, a vegetables drawer, a deli drawer, a shelf for leftovers (only!) and one for beverages. A place for everything and everything in its place. Just the way God intended.

I have a very hard time accepting any variation to the orderliness of my fridge.

When my parents roll into town they resemble something of a small tornado. Really they are more of a tsunami; a wall of destruction that brings with it more junk and stuff than you think could possibly exist in the world.

And for some reason most of that stuff ends up in the refrigerator: little canisters of creamer, old cups of coffee, random tea bags my father has been using for the past two weeks. Usually there is a Walmart bag or two (which when you put things in bags in the fridge it really obscures any hope of being able to categorize the contents. Come on, people!).

I live a pretty orderly life and, probably like most people, feel a bit unnerved when disruption comes into it.

Maybe this is why some people really hated Jesus. He brought disruption, He brought a new way of looking at things, a new way of looking at people. They were hoping for a military hero, they got a suffering servant. And people had a hard time with that.

Rejected and Chosen *(1 Peter 2:4-8)*

Choosing teams for a neighborhood game of baseball or football can be one of the defining moments of life for a kid. It kind of tells you where you stand, what your worth is. No one likes to be chosen last, or what's even worse, the odd man out. The exchange could go something like this:

"OK, we'll take Smith. You can have Jones *and* Dunham."

The little emphasis on "and" really means Dunham would not only not be an asset to our team, he would actually be a liability, and so it would be advantageous to us if he was on your side.

If you're lucky, the unfortunate team would accept you without too much public demonstration of their disappointment. The captain might say something like, "Well, you can be all-time center." Which basically means, "Hand me the ball when I say, 'Hike' and then get out of the way."

Or if you are less fortunate, the response might be, "Nah, you guys just take him. We will go with one less guy." Nothing quite like being the object of everyone's affection.

Rejection is a tough pill to swallow.

My wife left me about seven years ago. Told me I was a bad husband and that she never loved me. That was pretty rough. Makes you feel pretty worthless to be honest. Maybe she was right and I was a bad husband, and maybe she wasn't. The rejection is still the same.

I went to graduate school because, like anyone else who goes to graduate school, you have no other plan and you are just trying to put off life for a while. Well, not exactly. I had a little bit of a plan.

I was a philosophy student in undergrad, which I have been told is the same thing as majoring in pre-unemployment. And that's not far from the truth. I really didn't know what I wanted to do after school, so I worked for a year at a golf course mowing grass.

Being a greens keeper is highly motivational in that sitting on a lawnmower eight hours a day makes you realize that you don't want to mow grass for the next 40 years so you better get your butt in gear.

So an opportunity came up to go to Nepal with some family friends we had met in New Guinea some 15 years earlier.

I ended up at West Virginia University via Nepal. I was there working on a medical missions team, helping to build a hospital in a very rural, very poor part of the country. It was heartbreaking to know that kids were dying from simple things like diarrhea simply because they could not get clean drinking water.

WVU had a program in appropriate technology where you learn how to help communities like Chaur Jahari, Nepal develop safe water and sanitation systems and build their infrastructure in a sustainable way so that they can get themselves out of poverty. My plan was to get my master's degree then go back to Nepal to help my friends.

The program at West Virginia turned out to be a lot more theoretical and philosophical than I had originally thought, which I liked because I like philosophy and theory and all that. So I worked more on the theory of technology, its history and philosophy and how it impacts society and various social institutions. All very heady stuff that no one in Nepal would give two Rupees about.

I also met a girl, mentioned above, and got married.

So after six years at WVU, I pretty much had a doctorate in STS, (Science, Technology and Society), a wife and a daughter on the way. I needed to find a job.

To be honest I had no idea it was difficult to break into academia. I guess I figured my dad had done it somehow and I was pretty sure I was way smarter, better looking and more interesting than him. But apparently I was way wrong.

I think I must have applied to 30 jobs in STS from Harvard and Stanford all the way down to an online college run by some guy out of his garage in Dubuque. Not really, but you get the idea. I applied everywhere.

Not a single interview. No one even wanted to talk to me.

I'd like to think it is because they were intimidated by my spotless resume and stellar writing sample, but at some point you just have to admit that no one wants you.

That was a tough realization for me.

And two years later Amanda left and I had to start all over again. What is wrong with me? I am a reject of the worst kind.

The good news is that God is building His house out of rejects. Peter writes,

"As you come to him, the Living Stone--rejected by men but chosen by God and precious to him--you also, like living stones, are being built into a spiritual house to be a holy priesthood, offering spiritual sacrifices acceptable to God through Jesus Christ. For in Scripture it says:

"'See, I lay a stone in Zion,
    a chosen and precious cornerstone,
and the one who trusts in him
    will never be put to shame.'

50

"Now to you who believe, this stone is precious. But to those who do not believe,

"'The stone the builders rejected
has become the capstone.'" (2:4-7)

I honestly have no idea why God decided it would be a good idea to take the things that everyone else throws away, rejects, and use that stuff to build His spiritual house.

Of course, when I lived in Nepal they told me they would smear a mixture of cow dung and mud to stucco the walls of their houses. That made absolutely no sense to me until I saw how well it worked and how they used that crap (literally) to make their homes look really nice and well finished. Until you are *in* a culture you don't really get it.

It seriously blows my mind as to why the religious people in Jesus' day were so dense. Jesus was awesome: He was healing people, told great stories, could do all kinds of amazing miracles with fish and loaves and wind and waves.

What's not to like?

And yet they were constantly on His case, arguing with Him, trying to trick Him into saying something they could criticize (which they never could) and if that didn't work, they'd just try to throw Him off a cliff.

The thing is, Jesus kept talking about something that drove most people nuts. He kept talking about love and sacrifice and serving. The Jews lived under the thumb of the Roman empire. Everyone believed in an ethic of power and domination. That's just how things were done. You dominate those against you. You certainly don't love them and serve them, or die for them!

The religious leaders stumbled over that idea. The idea that what makes you great is a life of service and sacrifice and putting others first. A life of submission.

They could not accept that kind of Messiah and ultimately had to do what had always been God's chosen plan. They had to kill Him--the ultimate sign of rejection I would have to say.

I take great personal comfort in the fact that Jesus knows rejection way deeper than I do. His best friends left Him in His hour of greatest need. His own people murdered Him when He had done nothing but heal and teach and drive out demons and love people. It wasn't fair and it wasn't right, but it is the reality, and for my sake, it helps me understand and tolerate my own rejection.

And I am really glad that God has decided to build His house out of rejects. The ones no one else wants: the sinners, the tax-collectors, the sick, the weak, the poor and lame. Anyone who has experienced rejection, anyone with the courage to admit they are broken, has a place in the house of God.

"Jesus said to them, 'It is not the healthy who need a doctor, but the sick. I have not come to call the righteous, but sinners.'" (Mark 2:17)

Not a People *(1 Peter 2:9-10)*

I have never been literally homeless, but there are times when you travel that you feel like you may as well be. Every once in awhile you will find yourself in a situation where you have nowhere to go, no place where you can take off your pack and just relax for a while.

My family is pretty well known for hitting the road without really knowing where we are going. I mean, we have a general destination in mind, like Europe, but the specifics are usually worked out on the way. Things like cities and hotels and transportation are minor details that Mom and Dad don't seem to worry about until, well, until we need to worry about them.

I do not ever remember having a hotel reservation before we left for a trip with my family. Instead we would load up the family truckster with the hope of finding some unknown, off-the-beaten-track, secret location. Sometimes it worked, sometimes not so much.

There is an advantage to traveling without a predetermined itinerary: you are never tied down to have to be at a certain place at a certain time. You have great flexibility and you never *have to* be anywhere. If something or some place of interest catches your fancy, you can stay or move on. Whatever you want.

I remember one time coming across the little medieval walled-city of Rothenburg in Austria, I believe. We hadn't planned to even stay the night, but we happened upon it in the middle of some festival. The narrow cobblestone streets were packed with artisans and musicians, the whole town decked out in traditional garb. It was as if we had stepped back in the Middle Ages.

What was going to be a short visit turned into a few days. And it was great, a fortuitous find.

But then again when you travel by whimsy, you don't have a place to stay either, and that can present problems.

When I was in ninth grade, our family took a little trip to Mexico for Christmas break. While we did think we would end up in Acapulco eventually, my father thought it would be cool to touch down in Mexico City and see what happened after that.

As you may know, Mexico City is one of the most dangerous cities on the planet. Lots of gringos and white kids go missing or end up dead there. Unfortunately (or fortunately) we were apparently unaware of this fact (or maybe my dad was, who knows).

I don't remember where we stayed in Mexico City but I do remember leaving. Somehow in the massive metropolis we found the bus station--not the tourist bus station, with new, air-conditioned super buses--but the local bus station where it seemed like you had to have either a chicken or goat with you to get a ticket.

That was quite a trip over the mountains and through the deep valleys of Central Mexico. We stopped off for a few days in the very quaint, very cool city of Taxco. They mine tons of silver in the region I guess and the little village was full of silversmiths. Artists of all kinds lined the town plaza. That was a very enjoyable few days.

When we finally hopped back on the bus the only thing we knew is that we were going to Acapulco for the last couple days of our vacation. No hotel, no final destination, just six Americans following the winds of fate and chance.

As I said, sometimes this way of traveling is great, but sometimes it doesn't work out as well.

When we got into town, late morning if I remember correctly, we picked up our backpacks and started walking from the bus stop down the main road of hotels looking for a place we could stay the next few days.

One little problem with that plan was that half of the United States also decided that Acapulco would be a great place to go for Christmas. We could not find a room anywhere, and every place we checked the story was the same: "The entire town is booked because of the holiday."

It is not fair to say that we were homeless at that point. Truth be told we had not even spent one night out of doors, but there is a sinking feeling you get when you seem to be running out of options of places to go. You can sit in a hotel for a little while, cool off and catch your breath, but they are probably going to ask you to leave when they see you start to roll out your sleeping bag on the lobby couch and brush your teeth in the drinking fountain.

It is an unsettling feeling to not know where you are going to sleep, to not have a place where you feel like you belong.

We searched for hours, all day and into the night, looking for a place to stay. It is one of the most basic of human instincts. We have to find a place to sleep where we will be safe, where we can let down our guard, even if only for a little while.

At one point during the day, we even hired a taxi driver to help us look. He had a really small car (a VW beetle I think) that the six of us had to cram into. He drove us for hours, further and further north, trying to find a place, any place. There was literally no room at the inn and the sun was going down.

Sometimes, in those moments of feeling like you don't belong anywhere, it is really nice to just get a word of encouragement from somewhere. I remember our driver saying, "I may know a place where you can go."

I think Peter wants to give us a little assurance that we have a place to go when he writes:

"But you are a chosen people, a royal priesthood, a holy nation, a people belonging to God, that you may declare the praises of him who called you out of darkness and into his wonderful light. Once you were not a people, but now you are the people of God; once you had not received mercy, but now you have received mercy." (2:9-10)

There are tons of great little nuggets in those couple of sentences, but there are really two statements that jump out at me.

"You are a chosen people...a people belonging to God," and "Once you were not a people, but now you are the people of God."

It seems to me that Peter is reminding us that we have a place where we belong. We have a place that is home and that is with God. We belong to Him, to His house.

It is interesting that he mentions at one time this was not the case. At one time we did not belong to God, we were not a people. I take that to mean that there was a time when we were homeless, in a sense. We had no place to go, no place that we could call home.

But then something happened. God chose us. He picked us out of the crowd and said, "You now belong to me."

I think it is one of the amazing things of God that He is picking those who do not matter, who don't belong, and is bringing them into His family. He seems to like the homeless and the outcasts, the ones who don't seem to really have a family.

He stopped all the time to help someone no one else seemed to notice: a blind man on the side of the road, a sick woman lost in a mass of people.

In a sense we have all been that woman, alone, and lost in a sea of people. When I first came to West Virginia I was stepping into 25,000 students and I knew exactly no one. I had only been to the state once before, in the spring, and that was to visit. I felt very much alone until I stumbled upon a group of kids who were a part of Campus Crusade. They had an office in the student union. I remember stepping into that little cramped space (the office was maybe five feet by five feet) and into the middle of maybe six or so people. I thought I needed to take a chance:

"Hey, I'm Trey and I'm new here."

One guy spoke up: "Hey, I'm Jimmy!" He was completely bald except for one small patch of hair on his forehead that looked like a mustache. I was thinking, "Hey, you're weird! But I'm glad to know you."

There were others, a whole bunch of others actually: Billy Williams, Luke Harriman, Brian Mills, Stephen Beckwith, Dave Barker and many others who welcomed me into their little community, who told me in different ways that this was my new home, this is where I belonged. I have no doubt, though, that really it was God, working through those guys and people like Mark and Lauren and their little boys, and many more over the years, making a place, making me part of a people, His people.

It feels really good to know you belong somewhere , that you are part of a family and that you will always have a roof over your head.

Over the last couple of decades, I have learned that there are privileges to being part of a family, to belonging to a house, so to speak. You have a place to lay your head at night, a meal, clothing, and you get to go on vacation sometimes. But it also means you have things you have to do. In our house it was to pull dandelions, pick up dog poop and shovel snow. I am sure there were other tasks but those were the big three.

In the spiritual family there are things you get to do as well. You get to encourage one another and carry each other's burdens. You get to celebrate when others do well and cry when they don't.

You also have to work through issues and problems, you have to confront each other and be confronted. You can't just sweep things under the rug and avoid each other. I both love and hate that about my spiritual family.

Peter reminds us that God has chosen us to be His people, a new priesthood, to live and declare His values, His way of being in the world; out of darkness and into light. Priests are a special link, mediators and representatives between God and humanity; that is part of what it means to be in the house of God.

Our taxi driver drove us north out of the hustle and bustle of Acapulco. Slowly the large, concrete hotels and condos gave way to smaller wooden structures, villages with dirt roads, kids kicking a flattened soccer ball in the town square. A stray dog half-heartedly chased a chicken under an old wagon.

"This place is called Playa del Sol," his face now glowing from the light of the instrument panel. "This is the place I come from. This is my village."

He maneuvered through the narrow streets like someone who was home.

"My brother has a couple of small rooms that he will rent out to you. You can stay with us."

My father cleared his throat as if to protest, not wanting to intrude on this family, but to be honest we had no other option at that point than to find a bridge or a quiet spot on the beach to sleep.

"No, I insist," our driver responded before my dad could say anything, "we would love to have you stay with our family."

It was a generous invitation to some very weary and tired folks. Humbling and a little embarrassing it had come to this, but it was much appreciated. And we never felt so much at home as we did those few days in Playa del Sol.

Live Such Good Lives *(1 Peter 2:11-12)*

Like every kid, my parents occasionally embarrassed me. That's kind of part of the gig. In the case of my parents it was usually for trivial things like my dad wearing a teal green track suit that made him look like some kind of giant Easter egg, or my mother ordering hamburgers at McDonald's and asking for them to hold the bun. The BUN! Who does that?

Rarely have I stopped to consider if I have embarrassed them. I don't know that my parents were all that concerned with our family reputation, but I know that I did some pretty stupid things growing up (and as an adult). I have probably also done one or two things that have reflected well on them. The point being, whether I like it or not, what I do has an impact on the Dunham name, for good or bad.

For the life of me I cannot immediately think of a time when I truly embarrassed them. I did, however, grow up with three brothers and I can think of plenty of times when they brought some measure of shame to the family crest. So let's talk about that.

Where do I begin?

Jon and Joe were five and seven years younger than me, respectively. Being the younger set, they did not have the pressure of establishing the family name in junior high and high school that Tim and I bore. By the time we got through and they were entering secondary school, I like to think the Dunhams were well known for being articulate, athletic, academically adroit, socially adept and pretty good dressers. I'm not sure if that's true, but it's what I like to think.

Jon and Joe, riding the coattails of their older brothers' raging success, emerged from the pre-pubescent youth with what I would call and air of confidence. They were, after all, Dunhams, men of the world, younger siblings of Trey and Tim. Who wouldn't feel pretty good about that?

Confidence is a double-edged sword. It instills in you a freedom from the opinions of others, but it can, if wielded without discretion, lead to lapses in judgment. The other thing about confidence is that it is attractive. Jon and Joe soon became ringleaders of a small band of guys. "Hoodlums" is the term I believe my mother used.

Confidence and a following will lead you to push the boundaries of what is socially acceptable, and while I publicly cannot condone their behavior, privately I have to admit that most of their antics were pretty creative and funny.

One of their favorite activities was to go to romantic movies, usually when they had just come out in the theaters (to guarantee a large audience), but not before they had all eaten a very large and potent dinner, comprised primarily of beans. Beans, as you know, are also called the "musical fruit," and it was this gastronomic property which most interested my brothers.

Most romantic movies have an amorous climax where the leading man and lady lovingly embrace one another. For people who love romantic movies, this is the best, most anticipated moment in the film. It is this moment, the moment of the Big Kiss, when the film goer most closely relates to the characters on the screen, swept up in their story and their deep, passionate love for one another.

It is, coincidentally, the precise moment in which the bean symphony, heretofore percolating in the bowels of eight or nine high school boys, makes its triumphant and cacophonous entrance.

Not at all what the director of music intended as part of the movie soundtrack.

I have no idea who may have been sitting in the movie theater during one of those bean-driven episodes. But I know what they may have been thinking, especially the guy waiting for that moment to try to sneak in a little kiss with his girl.

Maybe not the best moment for the Dunham family name. Like I said, publicly I cannot approve of such behavior.

There was also the time when my father received a call in the middle of the night from the Laramie Police Department. On the other end was Joe, who had earlier in the evening gone "out" with seven or eight friends. Jon claims to this day he was "studying at the library," but we have our suspicions.

"Dad, we're in jail."

"Great. What happened?"

"Well, Jared broke a guy's windshield with a water balloon."

"A water balloon? How is that even possible?" My dad was a little more awake now.

"Exactly! These are trumped up charges! We think the corruption goes all the way to the top."

"OK, well I'm in bed. I'm not coming down there."

"That's all right, we are all pretty pumped to spend the night in the hoosegow."

"'Night, Joe."

Apparently, they had thought it would be fun (and harmless I assume) to toss water balloons at cars from Clint Devin's house on Alta Vista Drive. Clint had pretty good coverage at his place, the only problem was some of the guys couldn't throw (ahem, Jared) so they had to run out of the trees, revealing their location.

They only actually hit one vehicle all night. Jared launched a big sloppy balloon that, by some stroke of sheer luck, caught a small pickup square in the windshield. The driver slammed on his brakes and the boys scattered, some into the bushes on the side of Clint's house. Others dashed across the street to the seventh fairway of the Red Jacoby Golf Course and into a sand trap.

Nothing happened. The truck was motionless and no one got out, brake lights burned bright red in the deep Wyoming night. After a half minute or so the truck sped off down Alta Vista Drive.

The coast now clear, Joe and his friends emerged from their hiding places and slowly congregated on Clint's front lawn, recounting the incident, marveling that they had actually hit something.

They say most criminals are caught because they talk too much.

Not ten minutes later, three police cars careened around the corner and surrounded the Devins' front yard, locking all eight of the hoodlums in their search lights.

The next morning, Joe and his cohorts had to appear before the judge. Mom and Dad and the others parents were in the gallery when the boys entered. I wish I was kidding, but this is the honest truth: all eight were dressed in bright orange prison jump suits, hands and feet shackled to one another. A casual observer may have thought the most notorious gang of murderers had been apprehended, not a band of water-balloon-throwing delinquents.

After the trial, during which they were convicted of malicious ballooning, Mom and Dad brought Joe home. Jon was in the living room, innocently reading his Bible probably. My mother was not so convinced he had not somehow been involved:

"I wish they'd throw you in jail!" she blurted, with all the venom and vigor she could muster.

I wish I could say this was the only time my parents had the privilege of accompanying one of their sons to court, but it is not. But that is a story for another day.

I am sure there were many other times when we brought more than a little shame to the Dunham name. To be honest, when you are young and in high school, family honor is not all that important to you. You don't really think about how your actions affect your family, the impact they have. But you start to consider this more as you get older, not so much because you care about your own reputation, but because you realize it reflects on your parents, your brothers, your own kids.

Peter writes, "Dear friends, I urge you, as aliens and strangers in the world, to abstain from sinful desires, which war against your soul. Live such good lives among the pagans that, though they accuse you of doing wrong, they may see your good deeds and glorify God on the day he visits us." (2:11-12)

It is interesting to me that the goal of us living "good lives" is that people might see us and then think that God is pretty great. That is not what typically motivates someone to do well, so that someone else gets the credit.

Maybe that is why Peter reminds us once again that we are aliens and strangers. We are called to do things differently. We live well, we abstain, we do good, and God gets the credit.

That's what happens when we are part of a house, part of family. We reflect on one another. Good, bad or indifferent we are tied together and so it matters what we do, not only for our sake, but also for the sake of the family and the One whose name we bear. We carry the name of God. Which is a funny last name, but you get the point.

I should mention there is a more self-centered motive here as well, beyond just keeping up the family name. Peter writes that we should stop engaging in sinful things because those kinds of things "wage war" on your soul. I think that is pretty harsh imagery and I think Peter chooses it for a reason.

I think that sin, doing what is wrong when we know it is wrong, has a corrosive effect that is not always physical (but sometimes). It has a spiritual and emotional impact and is very real and tangible. Like cancer.

In *The Tell-Tale Heart,* Edgar Allen Poe examines the downward psychological spiral of a man who covers up a murder. Eventually he goes mad, confessing his crime when no one suspects him of any wrongdoing. The beating of the dead man's heart under his floorboards eventually becomes more than he can bear.

Call it guilt, call it conscience. A house that disintegrates from within doesn't really stand a chance.

My three brothers and I were all decent athletes in high school and won a few awards. I remember that at the senior banquet for my youngest brother, Joe, the coaches got my mother a trophy. It said, "The Wind Beneath Their Wings." That was a proud moment for me; I think maybe it was for her, too. We have her name and I am very proud that in some small way we brought honor to her.

JOIN THE CONVERSATION

Before you read the next chapter stop and read 1 Peter 2:13-25 and share what you think on Twitter at #Strangers&Aliens. I'd love to talk about what jumps out at you.

5 LIVING WITH RULERS
1 Peter 2:13-25

Most of us have had at least some experience with having someone else be in charge of us: a parent, a boss, a coach, a teacher, perhaps an older sibling. And I am sure we have all had good bosses and bad bosses, good coaches and bad coaches. And even if we had generally good parents, they weren't perfect and so you had to endure some truly unbelievable parenting from time to time. (I could tell some stories and probably will.)

Some of the best authorities in my life (aside from Mom and Dad--they really were great) were guys like Coach Deti. He was a short gnome of a man. He was the football coach at our high school for about 40 years. His father had been the coach for about 40 years before him. Our stadium is called Deti Stadium. He was P.E. teacher by day, and would roam the halls in sweats, muttering something about the single wing offense or something. He always had a stopwatch around his neck; his idea of a man necklace, I guess. Maybe he thought he might run into a new kid in the hall and want to check his 40-yard dash time.

He was unorthodox to be sure.

Coach Deti was my Driver's Ed teacher one summer and every day we'd go out to practice driving. The routine was always the same:

"OK, Dunham, let's practice driving to the dry cleaner. I have some stuff to pick up for the wife."

And then, "OK, Dunham, let's practice driving to the bank," or "Let's practice driving to the grocery store," and so on until the lesson was over and all of his errands had been run.

I heard from some other kids that Coach had taken a job delivering phones books in the summer, so they had a lot of practice driving "to the next house." On the last day we got to practice driving to the Daylight Donuts, where he met up with some of his old cronies to talk about the good ol' days of Laramie High football. He bought me a bear claw.

We all thought Coach was a little quirky, but we all loved him and would have done anything for him. Mostly because we knew that he really cared about us.

At the end of my sophomore year I was considering not going out for football. I had broken my arm that fall and didn't get to play much. To be honest, I didn't imagine I would get much of a shot to play the following year, so I figured I would just not go out and no one would notice.

One day as I was walking to class I saw Coach Deti coming down the hall opposite me. I just looked straight ahead not wanting to make eye contact, but he spied me. "Dunham, get over here."

"OK, Coach."

"Now, you get on out there for football next year."

"OK, Coach."

And that was it, I went out for the team. He was a good coach because he cared enough to find me and tell me (in his own weird, but charming way) that I was wanted and needed. Good coaches know when to do that. And good coaches are pretty easy to play for.

I have had other men who have spoken into my life over the years. My dad's good friend, Norm Tyser, was my boss at the sawmill. He told me I was slower than a snake's butt in December and I better pick up the pace. That hurt a little, but I appreciate now those words of instruction and encouragement. I use that phrase with some regularity now.

Gary Dodds was my boss at Dodds' Bootery, a family shoe store in my hometown. I worked there for a year after high school before our family moved to Europe for my dad's sabbatical. Toward the end of my tenure there, he noticed I was getting a little lax with my customer service and hustle. I remember him pulling me into his office in the back.

"Now, I know you're getting ready to leave and to go on your trip," he told me, "but you have a month left."

"Yes, sir."

"And I know you are ready to move, but you have to finish up well. It's only a month."

"Yes, sir."

"You can do anything for a month. You can eat a poop sandwich for a month."

I had never heard that expression before, but I got his meaning. And I appreciate the things I learned from Mr. Dodds in those months at the shoe store.

Good bosses are easy to work for, but we don't get good bosses all the time. By far my worst employment experience was the one day I worked at Arby's. My dad had been hassling me about getting a job and to quit laying around on his couch all day eating Cheetos or I'd have to start paying rent. So Arby's was the quickest thing I could find.

I was scheduled to start on Memorial Day for breakfast. (I know, who knew Arby's had breakfast?) Not many people, thankfully, because they might have gotten the weirdest sandwich ever if they had come on my first day.

I show up for work expecting to go through some sort of training and roast beef certification, but it was just me and the boss. He took one look at me and started digging in an old box in the corner.

"Here, put this on."

It was a crumpled up Arby's polo. I held it up and I am pretty sure it was a women's extra small.

"Do you have any other sizes?"

"Nope, that's it. Put it on." It was like a half shirt. Good thing this was the '80s.

OK, Boss, what's next? Like I said, I was expecting a little help in the fine art of roast beef culination. Help me just ease into this whole fast food business.

"You're on grill. We're cooking breakfast. I'll be on the register."

Wait a second! "How am I supposed to know what to cook?"

"Pictures of the food are on the wall. Eggs are in little fridge in the corner."

And with that he was off. I was left standing in a puddle of roast beef grease, holding a spatula and my shattered dreams of ever working fast food for more than one day.

I had no idea what I was doing, but I did my best. Fortunately only two customers came in that morning, the last two breakfast customers in the history of the Arby's franchise.

Peter tells us that one of the things we are going to have to do, one of the things that God expects from us is that we would be submissive to every authority, every leader that we have in our lives: a boss, a coach, a parent, whomever.

In our culture that is a pretty offensive and strange expectation. We are taught to question authority, to stand up for our rights, to assert ourselves and our own will. God just sees things working a little differently.

Actually, Peter points out that there are some really good reasons to do the right thing, to submit to authorities even when that authority may be unjust or incompetent, and to live submissive, respectful lives: it keeps people quiet, it earns respect and admiration, it relieves stress.

Observe.

The Ignorant Talk of Foolish Men *(1 Peter 2:13-17)*

I think we are by nature critical of others. We have, as a species, a real knack for finding, dissecting, explaining, analyzing, pontificating and pouncing on the weaknesses of pretty much everyone. I guess it all started in the Garden, when Adam pointed out that it was Eve who gave him the forbidden fruit. We have been quick to see the faults of others ever since.

This is especially true I think when it comes to people from other countries. It is easier to see things we can criticize because we just come from different worlds. I think I was in seventh grade when we had a French foreign exchange student, Philippe, come and live with us for a few months. I did not like that guy, probably because he complained all the time about what was wrong with America.

Another time, I remember my brother Tim and I were stopped at a checkpoint in Germany. We were driving that old Volkswagen bus of course, which admittedly had a few rust spots and still had a piece that cardboard in one window. And we did have to get out and push to get going because the starter didn't work, but all in all it wasn't a bad car. We made it home alive.

The border officer walked around slowly inspecting our vehicle, shaking his head. I thought he may have been looking for drugs, given that we fit the profile: two young Americans, haven't shaved or showered in a week, long hair, rumpled clothes.

After circling the van once, he looked right at me. I expected the worst.

"This is not a good car," he said with a kind of conviction that told me he really meant it. He may as well have thrown in, "And I think you are stupid Americans for driving it."

I was a little stunned by the critique. I am sure if you had seen the expression on my face as I strained to push and get that stupid bus rolling so we could pop the clutch and start the engine, you would have seen a look of disbelief.

It is rare that criticism comes at you so directly. More often than not it happens behind your back, or under the guise of hushed whispers and quick glances. When we lived in Budapest, we would hang out with Hungarian students quite a bit. I spoke practically none of the language.

Let me tell you, it is a very unnerving situation when everyone around you is laughing at some joke and you have no idea what was just said. For some reason I just always felt like it was about me. I was paranoid and insecure, sure, but I think those Hungarians had it out for me.

Several times I almost stood up in the middle of their laughter and yelled, "Oh yeah, well did you know that Hungary has never won a war and had their butts kicked all the way from China to Europe?! Huh? Laugh about that!"

I am glad I didn't in retrospect, but at the time it was all I could do to refrain.

I have no doubt that I have been the object of people's criticism over the years. Anyone who speaks at church knows that they are often the subject of Sunday dinner.

I had a friend tell me one time that he was mad at me for months after a sermon I gave on King David dancing naked as he brought God's Ark back to Jerusalem. My application point was that we should all get naked. Hold on a sec. By that I simply meant that there should be authenticity and transparency when it comes to our relationship with God.

He just heard, "Let's get naked!" There may be times and places for that kind of talk. Sunday morning church is apparently not one of them.

And he is my *friend*. Imagine what others had to say about me over their bucket of Kentucky Fried Chicken at lunch that day.

My natural impulse in these situations is to find something to criticize about those who are maligning me. We want to defend ourselves when we find ourselves to be the target of another person's criticism. I think that is a very natural reaction, a reaction everyone expects. When you poke someone you are kind of thinking they will take a swing back.

Peter writes to us suggesting a different way for the people of God, the people of His house. "For it is God's will that by doing good you should silence the ignorant talk of foolish men." (2:15)

What is interesting about what he says here is the suggestion that when we "do good" we somehow silence people. I think this is true in general. It is somewhat hard to criticize someone who is always doing nice things. I try this with my mother all the time and eventually it all just comes around to making fun of her because she is so nice. And that kind of takes all the fun out of it and usually just makes me feel worse about myself. And I don't know about you, but I deride people to feel *better* about myself, not worse.

Criticism of others is all about placing yourself above someone else. We tear others down because we think that will somehow make us feel superior, better, that it will elevate us in our own eyes and the eyes of everyone watching. Sometimes I am just dumb enough to think that this actually works.

I looked up what that phrase "doing good," means in the Greek and found something interesting. The word is *agathopoieo* and what it means literally is "to do something which profits others."

The context of this is Peter telling us that we should submit, place ourselves under in a voluntary manner, the authorities that God has put in our lives, whether they be kings or governors or whatever. It makes sense that we should put ourselves under those guys, they have a certain place and power in our society.

But Bob, my nosy neighbor, and Janice, his gossiping wife, are a different story. He's an insurance salesman and she works at the DMV. Lowlifes. Hard to imagine submitting to them or lowering myself to think about what I might do to profit them. Have you heard what they say about my lawn?

I think what Peter is suggesting is that by considering how we might do something which profits someone else (and then doing it), what we are really doing is shutting them up. When someone criticizes us and our reaction is to throw a punch back, the cycle perpetuates, punch after punch. But if we do good to them, if we figure out some way to profit them, it throws off their whole game.

It's like being in the boxing ring and you hand them a bouquet of flowers. There is not a lot you can say to that.

Nothing is as odd or quiets the criticism of others as quickly or thoroughly as one who considers the welfare of others first. It is really difficult to criticize someone who responds to harshness with love, to anger with kindness. Eventually you just run out of things to say.

Under the Pain *(1 Peter 2:18-22)*

I think my parents would tell you that I was a pretty good kid for the most part. I was compliant and obedient as far as I can remember. I don't think I ever got sent to the principal's office. I do remember having detention once in maybe eight or ninth grade, but I am pretty sure I was framed.

There were a few times, however, that I did some things that were a little uncalled for and for which I got punished.

The one that sticks out most clearly is the time I talked my brother Jon into kissing the girl who lived next door, Christy Bird, on the lips. He was probably four and I used sunflower seeds as my bait.

"All right, Jon, kiss her on the lips and I will give you a sunflower seed."

Jon would get a slightly embarrassed look on his face, kind of scoot over toward Christy, then all of a sudden grab her face with his two chubby little hands and plant one on her lips.

Jon was sheepish. She looked confused. I thought it was hilarious.

"OK, here's another one!" I was having the best time and I had a whole bag of seeds. Still chewing on the last little treat, Jon would again approach our dazed neighbor to begin again their awkward dance.

I was rolling, and probably would have kept going all day had not my father, the wet blanket of romance, shown up.

And he was not a happy camper.

That was back in the days when parents were pretty open about spanking their kids. He used a thin piece of lathe and it wasn't long before the whole neighborhood knew his stance on the sunflower seed kissing game.

And I have to admit, I deserved that one. And many, many of the punishments that came before and after that incident. I can accept that. I did the crime, I deserved the time.

What is much harder to accept is when we do what is right and still suffer for it. That kind of gets under our skin a little. We have a hard time tolerating the punishment and pain of the innocent. It doesn't seem fair, it doesn't seem just. And that is because it isn't.

But there is something very graceful and beautiful about the person who suffers for doing good. It is hard to explain how it is even possible, for someone who has been unjustly punished for just doing what is right, but even more inexplicable is the sense of awe and respect we have for those who do.

It is commendable, remarkable really, to both God and people, to follow the example of Christ: to suffer for doing good and to endure it. We may not understand it, but when someone suffers for doing the right thing, we respect that. Peter writes, "How is it to your credit if you receive a beating for doing wrong and endure it? But if you suffer for doing good and you endure it, this is commendable before God." (2:20)

When I was a kid, probably around 12 or 13, my parents bought a day care center. I was not old enough to be involved in the decision-making process for this particular investment otherwise I would have tried to talk some sense into them. My argument would have gone something like this:

"Kids are horrible, horrible creatures! Why else would parents want to drop them off at what basically amounts to a kennel for toddlers? Do not do this!"

I would have, of course, forgotten that I was still basically a kid and military school was still an option. What I didn't fully understand were the reason why my parents bought the day care center in the first place.

Bruce and Debbie had been longtime friends who had come on some hard economic times, but had found an opportunity. A preschool had come up for sale and if they could get the money together to buy it, they thought it could be very profitable. Enter Mom and Dad.

The arrangement (to the best of my knowledge) was that Bruce and Debbie were to be the operators of the child care center; they would run the business, manage the property and be in charge of the day-to-day. Our family was the investor. We provided the capital to get it going and I think my mother gave oversight to the accounting. My parents were involved to help their friends. That was the extent of their desire to be in the day care racket.

And in theory, their involvement was supposed to be minimal, just oversight and money. Nothing on the operational side. I liked that arrangement because it meant that my role was to stay home and watch cartoons on Saturday morning.

That is not even close to what actually happened.

I am not sure if it was anything specific, but it soon became very obvious that the business was going to fail if we didn't help. Lucky for my dad he had his own little crew of servants and for the next year or so my brothers and I became the janitors for the Sonshine House Day Care Center.

It was not as glamorous as it sounds.

The job entailed the mundane sweeping and mopping every night. Emptying the trash, putting up chairs and wiping down tables were not that bad. My adolescent sensibilities started to revolt, though, at having to scrub crayon marks off the floor and clean the bathrooms.

Thousands of tiny crayon marks covered the linoleum floor every night to the point that I wondered if we had run out of paper and the teachers just told the kids to go nuts. Every night Dad would issue us a cold, rusty piece of steel wool that felt like something you would pull out of your shower drain and some magical, invisible concoction he called "elbow grease." We would spread out, canvassing every room, crawling on hands and knees, moving from crayon mark to crayon mark, like soldiers belly-crawling a battlefield, till our bones ached.

Far worse was the bathroom. Any person who willingly scrubs surfaces that have been maliciously (I am sure) defaced by 25 three and four-year olds each day should be eligible for the Congressional Medal of Honor.

First of all those kids had no aim, and second, they had no conscience. There was a baseboard heater opposite the row of ankle high urinals in the boys bathroom. I have no doubt that was more often the intended target.

It goes without saying that we complained, my brothers and I, but our pleas for release were often met with two simple replies: "We are doing this to help out some friends!" and "You missed a spot."

So we swept, we mopped, we scrubbed, we cleaned. We pulled weeds in the playground out back. We mowed the lawn out front. We painted the outside of the building and we painted the inside. My mom would go in most days and help make lunch (thousands of peanut butter sandwiches cut in little triangles), do the books, and just help out wherever she could.

And still, despite our best efforts, the business failed. I don't know that it was anyone's fault; businesses fail all the time, and after maybe a year we had to close up the Sonshine House. My parents lost tens of thousands of dollars and ended up selling the business back to the lady they had bought it from.

And all they had done was try to do something nice for their friends. Sometimes you suffer for doing the right thing, for doing a good thing.

I think most people want to do the right and good thing, but the fact that you can sometimes suffer for it makes doing the wrong thing a little more enticing.

Some time ago, I came across a verse in Psalm 15 where David writes,

"Lord, who may dwell in you sanctuary?
  Who may live on your holy hill?
[T]hose who fear the Lord, who keeps his oath,
  even when it hurts." (1, 4)

That year or so we had the Sonshine House was difficult. It cost my parents a lot of money, and we had to work very hard to try to keep it going. Some people probably thought it was foolish to wager so much money on trying to help out friends, but I admire Mom and Dad for taking a chance to do good. I admire the fact that they went through with their commitment to help Bruce and Debbie and their family even though I am sure there were times it would have been much easier to walk away.

I think that it is highly unusual for someone to knowingly do right and understand that the end result might be a punishment of some sort: jail, embarrassment, financial ruin. We all know that doing evil may end that way, but to try to do good and know we can suffer and the result could be disastrous is a whole other ballgame.

There is no doubt that my parents suffered for helping Bruce and Debbie with this day care--we *all* did. They knew what could happen going in. They could lose a lot of money, and they did. But at the end of the day they did the best they could, they did the right and good thing to help out a friend. And as Peter says, that is commendable before God.

Entrusting Ourselves *(1 Peter 2:22-25)*

Aside from the normal wrestling matches that maybe got a little out of control with my brothers, I can only say that I have been in one fight. It was at football camp my sophomore year of high school. Matt Mesa stole the sports drink out of my mini-fridge and that was something I just could not let slide.

Tensions were pretty high that day. We had just finished our third practice on a dry, hot and dusty August afternoon. Camp Guernsey is a national guard training facility in the middle of nowhere; a collection of about 100 quonset huts set down on a patch of prairie thistles and dirt. Our practice field had about as much grass as the surface of the moon.

Rehydration was pretty critical and you didn't stand for anyone snaking your Kool-Aid from your fridge. That was crossing the line.

"Hey! Who took my orange drink?"

I looked over at the bunk across from mine. Matt Mesa was working on a gallon jug of cool, orange refreshment.

"Hey Mesa! Is that my drink?"

"Yeah, I guess it is," he said with surprising nonchalance.

"Did you take that out of my fridge?" I could feel the blood start to rise into my neck and ears.

"Yeah, I guess I did," he replied, putting the jug back to his lips and raising the container one more time.

I have thought about this incident quite a bit over the years, and I know what it was that made me jump into that fight: anger. That was it. Pure, unadulterated anger. There was an injustice in Hut Number 17 and it was not going to go unpunished. I looked around our bunk to see if I had any back up. Guys were making their way to their bunks to rest after the long practice. Others shuffled past us on their way to shower.

No one seemed to be paying attention to two skinny cornerbacks arguing over an orange drink.

Mesa was eye-ballin' me as if to say, "No one else cares. What'cha gonna do 'bout it?"

Something in my brain snapped, and I was off my bunk in a flash of fury. I knocked that drink out of his hand before he could swallow, and I started throwing haymakers as fast as I could.

I always imagined that I must have looked something like Muhammed

Ali, dancing, jabbing, landing an occasional left hook, the perfect picture of grace and power. The more likely scenario is me flailing about like one of those crazy inflatable tube men you see at car dealerships. I'd like to think I landed a punch somewhere in there, but to be honest I am not sure.

Someone pulled us apart after about 15 seconds. A small crowd had gathered. I heard from the back, "Was that Dunham attacking Mesa? What happened?"

"I think he stole his juice." This was met by a pretty healthy round of laughter, but soon it died out and everyone shuffled off to their bunks and their own cool drinks.

I sat fuming on my bunk for quite a while.

It has to be about the hardest thing on the planet to not retaliate when someone wrongs you, to not lash out or throw a punch when attacked. It is almost an involuntary response; when someone strikes out at us, we strike back. Maybe that was the surprising thing about the whole incident--my lunging and punching Matt felt so involuntary. I didn't plan it, it just happened.

I have never seen someone just let themselves get beaten up. I think that would be almost impossible. You would have to be from another world.

Peter writes, "When they hurled insults at (Jesus), he did not retaliate; when he suffered, he made no threats." (2:23)

It blows my mind to think about this. Jesus could have called down a whole army of angels and wiped out the entire place and yet He kept still. He let people spit on Him, beat Him, mock Him, tear His clothes from His body. He was humiliated and stripped naked, hammered to a cross, and in utter agony put on display for the entire world to see.

And He did not lift a finger.

The question that comes to my mind is how? How do you not do *something*? Jesus had all the power and ability to defend Himself and yet he refused to do anything. He took the punch.

I am mystified by this, I really am. How do you not defend yourself? It seems like such a basic human reaction.

Peter explains, "Instead, he entrusted himself to him who judges justly." (2:23)

Somehow, in the midst of all that pain, all that humiliation, Jesus believed and trusted that God was one who judges justly and that, in the end, all things would be made right. I don't know how He saw it in the moment, but He did, and this knowledge that God would defend Him-- judge rightly--released Jesus from the need to defend Himself.

There is something very freeing, I think, in coming to the conclusion that we do not have to stand up for ourselves. We do not have to defend ourselves when someone comes after us. We can trust God to defend us. There is a lot of pressure that comes with having to watch our back all the time. We can be consumed with questions like,

"Am I getting a fair deal?"

"Is that person trying to rip me off?"

"What if someone says something about me behind my back (or to my face)?

"If I don't look out for myself, who will?"

It can get really stressful when we feel like we have to be sure that no one is getting the best of us. We lay awake at night, worrying about what we might lose: a reputation, a client, some money, a promotion.

Or the other option is that we entrust ourselves to God, who judges righteously and maybe we can sleep at night.

This is totally counterintuitive, I know. Sounds a bit sissy-ish and naive, especially given our American ethic of power, something I think we share with the Roman Empire that dominated the world at the time of Jesus. But I think it works. And I think it is true.

God will defend us if we will stop our ridiculous attempts at defending ourselves. Like Moses told the Israelites as they fled from persecution in Egypt, "The LORD will fight for you; you need only to be still." (Exodus 14:14)

I was discussing this idea of not defending ourselves with a friend and he asked me, "Well, do you mean if someone hits me in the face, I shouldn't defend myself or hit back?"

And my answer was short, profound and full of conviction: "I don't know. Maybe."

At which point he punched me.

But it is a good question and one that I have wrestled with because to throw up our hands, to counterpunch, is so intuitive as to almost be beyond our control. I don't know if Jesus tried to deflect some of the blows He took, just from instinct, but from the text it seems His only defense was His trust that God would defend Him, God would stand up for Him and judge justly.

Maybe the irony is that I think it takes more strength and power to *not* react, to let someone get the upper hand. I think it was more a show of Jesus' strength, not His weakness, that He let everyone mock and spit on Him. Restraint, to me, seems more powerful because it is harder to maintain.

I think that is the beauty of the submissive life, the life where we do the right thing even though we suffer because of it, where we trust God to provide and look out for us in the midst of uncertain circumstances and under the authority of less than perfect people.

It is certainly not the normal way of doing things, but maybe that should tell us something.

JOIN THE CONVERSATION

Before you read the next chapter stop and read 1 Peter 3:1-7 and share what you think on Twitter at #Strangers&Aliens. I'd love to talk about what jumps out at you.

6 WIVES AND HUSBANDS
1 Peter 3:1-7

I was fortunate enough to grow up in a home where I had no doubt that my mother and father loved each other. I know this is not the case for everyone. I know that many people grew up in homes that were plagued with fighting and anger and violence. Moms and dads who said and did horrible things to each other and to their kids. Husbands and wives who gave up on each other because they couldn't figure out how to get along, or someone was too selfish to try. I hope that wasn't you, but statistics tell us that more than likely your parents are no longer together. And I am sorry for that. I truly am.

My parents will have been married for 47 years this coming December. That is a really long time to be with someone. I have lived with myself for 43 years and I am pretty much sick of it.

Few people probably know the story of their meeting. My parents met in May, I believe, of 1966, at a Campus Crusade for Christ meeting at Michigan State University. In the words of my father, "Most of us sat on the floor during the meeting, and that night I found myself in the front row opposite a very pretty girl in a blue dress with a full skirt gathered at the waist. She had short blond hair that was sort of 'puffy.' She had a great smile and I made eye contact with her a couple of times…. after the meeting I was up and across the room to introduce myself. I really don't remember much about our conversation, but I did manage to get her phone number. She recalls I kept calling her Sally." (The name of an old girlfriend.)

On their first date a few nights later, my mother fell asleep in the movie.

It is a little miraculous they got married at all.

Later that summer they ended up as counselors at a Salvation Army summer camp in upstate New York. On the way home, a whole summer after first meeting, my genius father decided it would be a good time to pop the question.

"(On the way home to Michigan) we drove the northern route so we could go to Niagara Falls and then through Canada on our way to Detroit. Sandy gave me a break and drove part of the way across Canada so I could get some rest. As I lay down in the back I asked her if she would marry me, to which she responded, "No." I imagine she pressed down a little harder on the accelerator at that point.

But to Dad's credit, he stayed with it. He wrote her letters all that fall and I guess eventually wore her down. Sometime around Thanksgiving that year, she wrote him and said she would marry him. They were married on December 30, 1966. Sometimes she thinks she should have stayed with her first instinct. No kidding.

I think they would be the first to tell you that they didn't do everything right. My mother has often said that she had no idea what she was getting into, but if she had…she trails off a little at that point. After some reflection she ends with, "It is not how I would recommend getting together with someone. We hardly knew each other."

But somehow they have made it work and there is something to be said for that. I think they'd be the first to tell you that they don't have the marriage thing all figured out, but there is obviously something about them that works.

They are both really stubborn for one. My mother was a farm girl from near Kalamazoo, Michigan. My father a gritty, undersized kid born without a left pectoral muscle (which he reminds us of incessantly to make sure his sons remember how much he had to overcome) from the small town of Clinton, Michigan. He recently wrote in his memoir that he once killed a chicken when he was about five or six, convinced he could get it to lay eggs by hitting it on the head with a hammer.

So they are tough people, if not all that bright, and I think that helps in marriage. You just kind of power through the rough spots until it gets better.

But my parents were very tender with each other, too. I can remember coming into the house on occasion (I was probably in high school, which makes it even worse) and they would be slow dancing in the kitchen, maybe smooching a little. Ugh, disgusting. "Get a room you two!" I would shout and storm off to my room, slamming the door, wondering what I did to deserve such punishment.

It was gross, but deep down you knew it was pretty cool that your parents were in love.

They had their fights, too, like any couple, but I do not really remember the details. I can remember once or twice the conversation getting a little loud and heated behind a closed door. And I recall seeing my mom crying a time or two. It was rare, but it happened.

The thing I noticed is that they always seemed to resolve things, one way or another, and that gave me a lot of confidence in them, in our family, that we would be all right.

Then again I am not sure my family has ever been "right."

When my dad retired he took up a strange hobby. He was a professor for 30 years or so and loved visiting various college campuses. Not long after leaving the University of Wyoming he decided he would buy a new car and he and my mother would visit every college in the United States. Literally. That is something like 3,000 schools I think, and hundreds of thousands of miles of driving.

I am not sure what mom thought of this idea, but she went along, and for several months things went pretty well and they had a good time.

Needless to say they spent a lot of time in the car and you can only talk so much, so my mother decided she needed something to help her pass the time. So she bought a little battery-operated keyboard that could rest on her lap and on which she could pound out her favorite hymns, mile after long and lonely mile.

I am not sure when the switch flipped for my dad, but eventually that little keyboard got under his skin. At the next rest stop he got her a "present": a nice set of headphones she could plug into her keyboard. He claims he was just looking out for her, wanting her to enjoy the rich tones of her Casio. Uh huh.

I am not sure that there is a single secret for wives and husbands to make a marriage work, but Peter hits on a couple things that make a lot of sense, character traits that I saw in my mother and father. And as I said, they've been together almost five decades.

The Unfading Beauty *(1 Peter 3:1-6)*

It is remarkable to me, as I have traveled, how different cultures view beauty in different ways. What I mean is that the characteristics and traits that are considered to make one beautiful are often different, even opposite, from one country to another.

When I was in Nepal, I lived in a medium-sized village called Chaur Jahari. Most of the families were very poor, subsistence farmers at best. The women worked incredibly hard. Daily they had to cook for the family, finding a way to make a cup of rice and lentils stretch for six people.

Homes in Nepal were made of stacked rock held together with a mortar made from mud and cow dung. Floors were almost universally dirt. Imagine trying to keep that place clean and sanitized. Not enough Purel on the planet.

In the morning you would often see groups of mothers and daughters carrying laundry down the steep 300-foot high trail to the river to wash clothes, beating them against the rocks.

And every day I would see scores of women and girls returning from hours-long treks to the far reaches of the district to find cooking and heating wood and water. They would stack dozens of branches and five-gallon buckets on their heads, sometimes needing to travel 10 miles round-trip to find these basic necessities.

I cannot really overstate how difficult life was there for women and how hard they worked to survive. It was impressive.

To be fair, the guys worked, too. They had to try to grow some food from the rock-hard red clay that covered our little valley. They would wrestle their water buffalo (if they were lucky enough to own one) or pound the ground by hand with a hoe (if they were not so fortunate). In a good year they could feed their family, but not every year was a good year.

Farming in Nepal is kind of a part-time gig. Once seed is in the ground you wait for it to grow and pray for rain. And so most days the guys did not have much to do. I was usually pretty busy with things I needed to do for the clinic and hospital, but occasionally I would get some time to sit with the boys and people watch.

Dal Bhir was a thin, hard, sinewy man, like just about everyone in Chaur Jahari. He looked to be 50, but was more likely in his early 30s. A life of manual labor and poor nutrition will do that to anyone.

He was kind and could put up with my broken Nepali, so we would sit together sipping chai, watching folks wander past.

I remember one afternoon a large and what appeared to be very important woman passed by. She had on a vibrant sari, made from very fine silk. It shimmered like water in the sun as she moved. Her hips rolled like a cargo ship on the sea, swell after swell. I started to get a little sea sick.

Her fingers were plump, adorned conspicuously with multiple ornate, bejeweled rings, like the bands on a fistful of giant cigars. In one hand she carried a light pink parasol to shade her massive head; in the other a sausage, partially eaten.

I turned to pick up my cup to sip a bit of chai to try to ease my stomach, and as I turned I caught a glimpse of Dal Bhir's face. His eyes were transfixed on the woman.

"Wow!" he whispered, more to himself than me.

"Excuse me?" I replied, trying to cover the surprise.

"She's beautiful."

"Who?" I responded, thinking I may have missed someone else hidden or perhaps caught in the gravitational orbit of this massive woman. But there was no one else around.

"Who, her?" I asked for clarification.

"Yeah, she is so fat! What a hottie!"

So I am loosely translating there, but that was the gist of it. He really, truly thought she was beautiful, and basically he thought this because she was chubby. I didn't see it (literally). But he was into her, that I could not deny.

I would learn later that you only got to be overweight in Nepal if you had money. Only the very rich can afford enough food, good food, to put on any extra weight.

And so I think maybe subconsciously this is what my friend was experiencing and why she was becoming to him. His attraction for her, although very much tied to her physical appearance on one level, was rooted to a deeper reality about this woman. She had money. And guys like money. Girls do, too.

The point is simply this: what we perceive as beautiful is ultimately tied to something beyond just the physical appearance. Beauty, I think, is the embodiment of a deeper set of values. For Dal Bhir, this woman was physically beautiful because she was wealthy. What I learned that day is that beauty is not empirically objective, it is in the eye (and values) of the beholder.

It is probably not all that different for Americans. I wonder if there is a direct correlation between the perceived beauty of a woman (or man) and their wealth. I have no data to support this idea, but I would be interested to know.

I am no female psychologist, but I am pretty sure every woman wants to be thought of as beautiful, especially by her husband. Usually they go about achieving beauty by hair and makeup and a wide assortment of creams and ointments, a membership to the gym and a few hundreds visits to the mall for clothes. In extreme cases, people will even go to the plastic surgeon, hoping a new nose or a flatter stomach or a rounder caboose will help.

I'm not judging; I get it. I want to look good, too. I look in the mirror pretty much every day. I am trying to lose a few pounds right now, which, if I am honest, is less about my health and more about me not looking like a marshmallow at the pool this summer.

It is a part of our culture that is hard to escape. And I think that is what makes Peter's suggestions on beauty hard to really understand.

Peter writes that a woman is beautiful not because of how she looks or does her hair or the clothes she wears, but because of her gentle and quiet spirit.

"For this is the way the holy women of the past who put their hope in God used to make themselves beautiful. They were submissive to their own husband, like Sarah, who obeyed Abraham and called him her master. You are her daughters if you do what is right and do not give way to fear." (3:5-6)

Peter obviously did not live in the good ol' USA in 2013. There are probably few things written that are more offensive and foreign to our culture than the idea of a submissive wife. Want to get punched in the nose? Tell the average woman to submit. Ain't gonna be pretty.

But I think that the beauty of submission is something that largely goes misunderstood in our culture. The idea in the original language is to voluntarily put yourself under the leadership of another. "Hupotasso" is a Greek military term meaning "to arrange [troop divisions] in a military fashion under the command of a leader." In non-military use, it was "a voluntary attitude of giving in, cooperating, assuming responsibility, and carrying a burden."

Peter is writing about the time when Abraham and Sarah were following God to a new home that He had promised them. On the way they ran into some powerful men and Abraham was freaked out that they may kill him and take his wife because Sarah was so good looking.

Sarah went along with Abraham's lame brain plan to tell everyone she was his sister and not his wife. Of course even though it (possibly) saved Abraham's life, this dumb idea opened the door for these kings to take Sarah as their own wife. God had to step in twice to protect her chastity. God's plan was that Abraham and Sarah would be the parents of a great nation and He couldn't have some other guy possibly messing up the works.

I think what makes Sarah so beautiful is not so much that she submitted to her husband, but that she trusted God. She believed that God would protect her and make a way. And her trust in God was reflected in her willingness to let Abraham lead. I think she knew Abraham's plan was a bad idea, but she also knew that she could count on God. Beautiful.

It does wonders for a man's confidence to know that his woman will stand by him, support him, believe in him and even let him make mistakes when she knows better. Men will go to battle for a girl who respects him; maybe she doesn't always agree with him, but if she shows respect nonetheless, that is a pretty amazing thing. It doesn't get much more attractive than a supportive wife.

When I think of my mom, I think this is how Sarah must have been. Sandy Dunham has strong opinions to be sure, and she shares them, but she respects my dad, lets him lead. She has maybe the most quiet and gentle spirit of any woman I have ever known, and she has wielded that quiet spirit like a sledgehammer (metaphorically speaking) when it comes to dealing with my dad--very effective. Lord knows, he has made mistakes and probably made moves she disagreed with, but she trusted God with the result and she has stood by him through them all. And that's both impressive and beautiful.

Consider as You Live *(1 Peter 3:7)*

Not long after we moved into our grass and bamboo house in New Guinea, our family was invited to attend the wedding of a local village girl to a young man who lived the next valley over. Weddings are a big deal pretty much everywhere, and the Kinona Valley is no exception.

The ceremony was (as I recall) about a three-day affair, but had many of the same characteristics as our American weddings: there were two parties, the bride and her family on one side, the groom and his crew on the other. Everyone dressed very fancy, which meant lots of traditional headdresses and grass skirts and the ever-present pig tusk through the septum of the nose.

The men got out their best bows, arrows and axes, which is something I think American weddings lack and would seriously raise the level of excitement with all the uncles drinking way too much and then proposing a challenge to see who could knock the little plastic bride and groom off the cake from 50 yards. (I'm just saying I would want to be at that wedding.)

There was also a lot of dancing. In New Guinea, they do not have a DJ per se, but there is one guy who does a lot of yelling, and that seems to get people going. Lots of people bring their own drums and everyone sings. What they lack in musical tone, they more than make up for in volume. It doesn't matter what note you sing as long as you sing it as loud as you can.

The groom always arrives with a huge entourage to the bride's home village. Everyone is decked out and excited trying to make a good impression. There is a lot of yelling and chattering of bowstrings against arrows. The groom is here to get his bride and he wants the world to know it. It is quite impressive.

Before that can happen, though, there is the matter of the bride price. I think that most of this is arranged prior to the actual wedding, but the bride's father and groom's father sit down and discuss the price which the groom's family must pay for the girl.

She must be bought with a price.

I will skip for now the obvious allusions to Christ coming for his bride and the price that was paid for her. I have no idea of the origination of these traditions in New Guinea, but the whole thing was almost identical to what I experienced at weddings in Nepal. It strikes me as more than coincidental that two such remote cultures would have such a similar and, quite frankly, biblical understanding of weddings and marriage.

The whole bride price was something very new and interesting to me. I had never heard of such a thing back home. We do, of course, give gifts to the couple, usually a toaster or set of bath towels to get them started. I had never heard of the groom's family paying the bride's father. In fact, the bride's family usually foots the bill for the majority of the shindig.

As we entered the village, I noticed about 30 pigs tied to nearby fence. They all looked a bit like, "What are *we* doing here?"

The process of the bride price is pretty simple: the two families must come to an agreement on what the young bride is worth. As I understand it this was based on two primary criteria: how productive was she in the garden and how many kids did they think she would have.

Hardworking, childbearing women could fetch upwards of 100 pigs.

The bride was not a part of this discussion. She had no say in the matter and I can only imagine how it must have felt to know your father was basically selling you to someone else.

It is always sad when a human being is objectified and treated like a thing, like something you own, but I had never witnessed exploitation so brazen, blatant and explicit as this.

Women in New Guinea and in many places around the world are viewed as no more than property, an investment commodity useful for growing and increasing one's personal wealth. It is a sad reality, though, and I remember a few times beaten wives showing up to our door in the middle of the night, my mother helping treat the bruises and lacerations inflicted by a drunk or angry husband, and a culture that considered these wives as nothing more than a piece of equipment.

Needless to say this is not how God views women or intended for the marriage relationship to work. Peter outlines a different way for men to view their wives:

"Husbands, in the same way be considerate as you live with your wives, and treat them with respect as the weaker partner and as heirs with you of the gracious gift of life, so that nothing will hinder your prayers." (3:7)

First of all I am no theologian, but I think his use of the word "weaker" is a really unfortunate translation of the word "poieo." This word is translated literally dozens of ways, but the overriding sense is "to produce, or bear."

What I think Peter is getting at here is that men need to understand the fact this person is part of you. Eve was "produced" or borne from Adam's very side, so he needs to think of her as a literal part of him. Genesis says that "a man shall leave his father and his mother, and be joined to his wife; and they shall become *one flesh*." (2:24, emphasis added)

And men would probably do well to remember who bore them.

I think it drives anyone crazy when they think they are not being heard or listened to. Being ignored is one of the most annoying things in the world. I know, I have a nine-year old daughter.

The Bible is full of examples that show the wisdom of listening to others, seeking advice, considering other opinions. Even God Himself listened to Moses' advice and didn't wipe out the Israelites who were pestering Him to death with all their moaning and groaning and complaining. Moses argued that it wouldn't reflect well on God's name if he wiped out His own people. He thought about it and basically said, "Eh, you have a point."

I am no expert on the female psyche, but I have noticed that women like to talk and process things verbally. They have an innate need to share things like feelings and emotions and opinions and what do you think about my haircut and did I tell you the Smiths got a new dog and I am not sure that is a good idea with the little baby, etc., etc.

Men are not really wired this way. We usually work things out by ourselves in our head and then act. It is the reason things get done in the world, and simultaneously the reason the world is such a mess. We don't listen.

I have also noticed that women see the world in a very different way than men, and that they have a perspective that is insightful, helpful and usually right.

A few years ago at the church where I worked, a goat got away from the annual live nativity scene and was running amok in the streets. Somehow the local paper got wind of this and called the office to find out what was being done to corral this menace/endangered pet. (They hadn't quite landed on what angle they were going to take with the story.) My friend Lauren was the communication director at the time and assured the hounding reporters that our people were out looking for the runaway and things should be under control soon.

As she was hanging up the phone, her husband, Mark, the high school pastor, strode into her office with three students following close behind. In their hands they each held a fully-loaded, semi-automatic paintball gun from the previous week's youth outing.

"Hey, we heard the goat got out!" Mark said with a little too much enthusiasm.

"Yes," his wife replied slowly. She knew her husband well enough to be more than a little concerned with where this might be going.

"So we thought we'd go track it down," Mark said, adjusting his camo bandana.

"With paintball guns?"

"Well, you never know when a situation might turn ugly." He said that last bit with a little too much of a smile on his face. It was evident that in his mind the situation had already gotten ugly. They knew what they had to do.

"Hmm. OK. Well, as your wife, I would just like to say that I think it might be a bad idea to shoot a scared little goat with paintballs. In public.

With kids. Without parental permission."

The manboys stood firm, but inwardly started to wonder if there was something they might be missing in this scenario.

"And secondly, no. As the communication director for this church, you absolutely may not go shoot that goat."

The newspaper was already out looking for it, and the last thing she needed was a front page photo of her husband and three high schoolers engaged in some sort of standoff with a paint-splattered barnyard animal.

To his credit, Mark was smart enough to listen to his wife. Slowly they all lowered their weapons, turned, and shuffled out the same way they came in.

Peter says the husband is to *consider* her. Listen to her, include her in the process, and think about what she has to say. It is a fool who does not listen to counsel, who does not take into account the advice given by others.

She is an heir with you, she is part of you. Listen to her. I think this is why Peter throws in that part about your prayers not being hindered. You don't listen to your wife, so why would God listen to you?

There is no doubt my father was the leader in our family, but it is equally clear that mom was his chief counsel. I know that they would spend many hours discussing and considering together what to do and how to lead our family. I know that he considered her, listened to her and valued what she had to say. And I am sure that played no small role in their success as husband and wife.

JOIN THE CONVERSATION

Before you read the next chapter stop and read 1 Peter 3:8-22 and share what you think on Twitter at #Strangers&Aliens. I'd love to talk about what jumps out at you.

7 TO SUFFER FOR GOOD
1 Peter 3:8-22

When I was a year or so out of college, I had the opportunity to move to Nepal and work with a medical missions team in the rural, western district of Rukum. Nepal is easily one of the poorest countries in the world. Kathmandu is comprised mainly of slums, row upon row of cardboard and sheet metal shacks. Many families make their living rummaging through the massive garbage piles on the outskirts of the city, hoping to find some food or other useful item they can sell, just hoping to make it through another day.

Kids die there from ridiculous diseases. Diarrhea is the number one cause of death for kids under five in Nepal. Infections from simple cuts and scrapes that could easily be cleared up with a little triple-antibiotic ointment are allowed to fester untreated, leading to unnecessary pain and sometimes death. Leprosy is a very real problem; I saw men and women, the ends of their hands and feet raw and bleeding where fingers and toes should have been.

Nepal can be a very sad place and I was incredibly blessed to get to go and try to help out some.

As I've mentioned, I lived in a very small village called Chaur Jahari. There were no roads to this town nestled in the shadow of the Himalayas, only a footpath, and if you were wealthy and patient, you could catch the weekly flight that came in and out on a single engine Air Nepal airplane. I call it an airplane only because that is the technical name. In reality, it was no more than a tin can the size of a single bed to which someone had attached what I think were a couple of pieces of plywood for wings and a lawnmower engine.

The landing strip was, for 6 days and 23 ½ hours of the week, a grassy meadow kept neatly trimmed by local water buffalo and goats. I made four flights coming and going from Chaur Jahari, each one delayed by stubborn or just plain ignorant livestock.

Ironic as it may seem given the setting, there was a terminal at this airport. To the side of the strip stood a small stone and mud structure about the size of the average American garage. Inside, a representative of Air Nepal was present to serve as baggage handler, mechanic (whose services were often required), concierge and customs and immigration as needed. (Hint: it was always needed.)

I didn't realize it until I had been in Chaur Jahari for a while, but there was a great deal of community and civic pride in this modest airport. It represented a certain level of sophistication and civilization for the members of this small outpost. It was their connection to a much bigger world and the weekly flights reminded them of their importance and significance. At the sound of the plane's coughing and choking engine coming from behind one of the mountains, children and adults alike would drop their toys and tools and run to the edge of the strip, eagerly awaiting the plane and the contents it contained.

One of the facts of being an American in this kind of setting is that you are by default a celebrity. This has nothing to do with who you actually are and everything to do with the perception most people have of the United States, i.e., that we are all on television, extremely wealthy (which we are in comparison to most of the world) and live in Hollywood. It was an unavoidable fact that as a big, (hey, it's all relative) goofy white guy, I was going to draw some attention, and throughout my time there I usually had a pack of boys following me wherever I went. People used to joke that they could tell which house I was in by the crowd gathered outside.

Being part of a medical mission team, our goal was to build a hospital for the district. There was literally no medical help available for hundreds of miles. While construction was in process we ran a small day clinic to help out as best we could.

The clinic was a stone and mud three-room building with hardly any supplies, a single doctor and one nurse, but folks would walk for three or four days, often carrying sick and injured loved ones, in hopes of getting help. We had a small waiting area outside the clinic where people could sleep at night until the clinic opened in the morning. It wasn't unusual for the staff of one doctor and one nurse to see over a hundred people per day.

The need was great and we didn't have much, but we worked hard and did what we could. People knew that they could come and get help and that we would try our best. Foreigners were not welcome long-term in Nepal, but because of the help we were trying to bring we could obtain 12-month visas, sometimes more.

I am telling you this not to be self-congratulatory, but to set some context for what happened on my way home from Chaur Jahari back to the United States.

I had been living in the village for nearly a year at this point, and I am pretty sure I knew every man woman and child by name. We had gone to several weddings and funerals and celebrated holidays with many of them. We had shared many meals together. Every Sunday I cooked lunch for a different group of boys, usually pancakes, which they didn't really get or like, but it was easy.

The point is, I knew these people and they knew me, which made my departure from Chaur Jahari International Airport strange, offensive even, and caught me so off guard.

The day I left our small village in the Himalayas was very sad, filled with many hugs and tears and gifts and promises to write, etc. I was a little emotional and reflective, remembering all the things we had done, the help and love we had tried to show, the friendship and lifelong bond we would share.

I lugged my backpack into the "terminal" and placed it on the low table in the middle of the room. I had my ticket in hand--a handwritten note from one of the village elders--which I gave to the ticket agent, Laksmi. I had made her son pancakes a few weeks earlier. I was the only passenger that day.

Laksmi looked at my ticket, then looked at me, then back down at the ticket. Her face stern and serious.

"Can I see your passport?" she asked. My Nepali was about at the level of a five-year old so I asked her to repeat the question because I thought maybe I heard wrong.

"I must see your passport," she repeated a little more sternly.

"OK," I replied, opening the top of my pack and digging for it. I hadn't thought I would need it at this point in the trip.

"Here you go," I said, a little confused by the formality of the situation. She examined my documents, looking first at the passport and then at me and then at the passport and back at me as if to make sure I wasn't in disguise or something. This was weird.

"Open your baggage."

"Huh?"

"Open your baggage. I have to search."

"You have to search? I was at your son's birthday party last month. What could you possibly think I would be smuggling?"

"I have to search."

I have been through a lot of airport security in my life, but never as thorough as that one. She literally pulled everything out of my bag. At one point they took a stick and shoved it in my tube of toothpaste to see if I had something stashed in there. I was dumbstruck. I had nothing to say.

I know she was only doing her job, but I was a little put off. We had been working tirelessly to help Laksmi and her people. I just didn't get the distrust. I felt a little insulted, disrespected. In all honesty it made me a little angry, and for a moment or two I had the thought, "Well, why don't you just build your own hospital then, if that's how you are going to treat people trying to do a good thing here."

When the search was over, my entire bag was unpacked, underwear, toiletries, socks, everything strewn across the table between Laksmi and myself. A small crowd had gathered outside and was peering in the window.

"Find anything?" I asked like some smart aleck fifth-grader. She didn't understand English, but she got the tone. No one moved for a couple of minutes.

And when it became apparent that my bag was not going to repack itself, I started grabbing and violently shoving whatever I could reach back into my pack. All the while I muttered and groused every insult I could think of, my eyes locked in a tight stare with Laksmi's.

The crowd sensed the tension and the intent of my rant: to humiliate this person who had humiliated me. I think it worked.

I suppose that is a natural reaction, but not one that I am very proud of.

For some reason our natural inclination is to repay an insult with an insult, but Peter reminds us that this is what makes us strange, this is what makes the people of God different: we should not repay evil with evil or insult with an insult, but rather we should repay those things with a blessing.

Repaying Evil With Evil *(1 Peter 3:8-12)*

There is no doubt that different cultures respond to situations in different ways. Sometimes as Americans we expect the world to react to incidents and crises the same way we do, but often that is not the case. And that can be both confusing and frustrating.

I worked at a small mission high school in New Guinea the two summers after my year in Nepal. New Guinea has around 700 unique languages, so when the country gained its independence they (lucky for me) adopted English as the official language for the country. So kids in school learn to speak English, often more properly than a lazy native speaker like myself. The result was confusion to be sure.

I remember numerous conversations that went something like this:

"Hey, Tom Tange, do you want to go with us to play some rugby?" I would ask.

"No, thank you."

"OK, so you don't want to go?" with a slight inflection to be sure he knew we really wanted him to join us.

"Yes," would be the response.

"Wait, so you want to play rugby with us?"

"No."

"Right, so you don't want to play?"

"Yes."

"What?!" At this point I would start looking around for someone to translate from English for me.

What it took me some time to figure out is that he was agreeing with my statement, "Yes, I do not want to play rugby." That is NOT how we do it in America, son! We double up on that negative (or even triple if we really mean it), "No, I don't want to play no rugby and in America we play a real man's game and it's called football!"

Nepal was even more strange. It took me months to figure out that when people nod their head they mean "no" and when they shake it they mean "yes." I wondered why we seemed to always have such a hard time getting on the same page with things!

Life gets weird when people respond in a way opposite to what you expect.

In terms of strangeness or clash of culture it gets no more pronounced than the command to repay evil or insult with a blessing, or to believe that kind of response will result in a blessing. Peter writes, "Do not repay evil with evil or insult with insult, but with blessing, because to this you were called so that you may inherit a blessing." (3:9)

I just am in the middle of studying Genesis with my small group and we came across the passage where Jacob stole Esau's blessing. I did a little research and found out that what he stole was Esau's rightful position as the eldest son, as the patriarch of the family. What Jacob received from his father, albeit dishonestly, was authority. When one considers that meaning of the word blessing, it gives a new twist to Peter's suggestion.

So here is what I think Peter is saying: when someone brings some kind of evil against you or they insult you, instead or repaying that with evil or another insult, give that person a blessing, which means to give them a place of honor and authority in your life. In other words, submit to them, place yourself under them in the same way soldiers fall in line and place themselves under the authority of a commanding officer.

This is of course a totally counterintuitive response. Common wisdom says that if someone puts you down or does something to harm you, you need to retaliate, make sure you are not taken advantage of. The last thing that is natural is to *respect* and submit to someone who insults and injures you.

To be honest I do not really get why God wants us to act this way other than to say that is just how things work in His kingdom. Peter writes, "to this you were called so that you may inherit a blessing." (3:9)

Calling has to do with your name, or rather the name that you bear. And Christians bear the name of Jesus, the name of God, so we do things the way He lines them out. Even if it doesn't make complete sense.

I don't think Jesus always totally understood why He had to bear the insults and injury of His own people, why He had to suffer and die when He could have easily called down a legion or two of angels in retaliation. I mean He *knew* why, I think He was just hoping there in the garden that there might be another way.

I had to do a lot of things that my dad asked even though they made absolutely no sense to my adolescent mind. He had his reasons, though, I'm sure.

The really curious thing about all this is the promise that God makes. The result of repaying insult and injury with a blessing is ultimately a blessing of our own. Our inheritance is a place of honor.

I think Paul does a great job of explaining how Christ exemplifies this kind of behavior in his letter to the Philippians:

"Your attitude should be the same as that of Christ Jesus:

"Who, being in very nature God,
  did not consider equality with God something to be grasped,
 but made himself nothing,
  taking the very nature of a servant,
  being made in human likeness
"And being found in appearance as a man,
  he humbled himself
  and became obedient to death--even death on a cross!
"Therefore God exalted him to the highest place
  and gave him the name that is above every name,

that at the name of Jesus every knee should bow,
in heaven and on earth and under the earth,
and every tongue confess that Jesus Christ is Lord,
to the glory of God the Father." (2:5-11)

God promises that those who return a blessing for evil and insult will themselves receive a blessing. It's not really what you expect. He is very clear that it is because Christ was obedient, died amid insult and injury, that He is now seated with a blessing, in the highest place, above every name, with all authority and power and glory.

And in a letter to the church at Ephesus, Paul writes, "God raised us up with Christ and seated us with him in the heavenly realms." (2:6)

What this means may not make sense, but it is true and it is something to believe in. "Do not repay evil with evil or insult with insult, but with blessing, because to this you were called so that you may inherit a blessing." (3:9)

Fearing What They Fear *(1 Peter 3:13-17)*

I think most of us are afraid of getting taken advantage of. There's just something about our humanness that makes us react almost instinctively when we find ourselves in those kinds of situations.

When I was about 13 or 14 my family took a trip to Mexico. I remember being on a very packed bus somewhere in Mexico City. My three brothers, my mother and I got a little separated from my father who stood more in the middle of the bus. We ended up at the back but could see him through the crowd.

For about the first 25 minutes it was a normal bus ride--people bouncing up and down, swaying to and fro with the motion of the bus as it made its way through traffic. You bump into people from time to time, but that is just part of the experience. No big deal.

I was falling into a sort of hypnotic trance from the drone of the engine, the warmth and gentle rocking of the cabin.

Suddenly I was jolted wide awake from the sounds of what seemed to be a fight erupting in the bus. I hoped it wasn't what I thought it was going to be, but I looked up and sure enough, my father was throwing haymakers at anyone within arm's reach.

The bus stopped and confused/slightly injured Mexicans poured out of the now open doors.

"Dunhams, out!" bellowed my father's very distinct, strong voice.

Still unaware as to what was going on, we obliged and soon we all stood perplexed and alone on the sidewalk, the bus now leaving the curb.

"What in the world happened?" I think it was my mother who asked.

Dad was frantically scanning the now dissipating crowd, his face a little red, eyes crazy from the sudden rush of adrenaline.

"I got pick-pocketed!" he gasped. "But I think I landed a couple good shots on the guy."

As funny as the scene was to us, and maybe ridiculous, I think we all react in the same way when we find ourselves in harm's way, when we find that someone is trying to cheat us or take advantage.

I think our fear is that they are going to get away with it. We're afraid that God is not going to come to our rescue.

That was Cain's fear. He abandoned God, even after God put His mark on His forehead, because Cain was afraid that he was going to be killed. Because he found himself in this vulnerable state, he went and built up some defenses, a walled city.

Before we go bashing Cain, or my dad for that matter, it makes sense, doesn't it? We protect ourselves. Someone throws a punch, you put up your hands, and then you punch back. It is deeply ingrained in us.

Most people fear what will happen if they do not retaliate when wronged. We live by the old saying, "If you don't stand up for yourself, nobody will." This sounds like wisdom and good words to live by, but again, for strangers and aliens in the world Peter suggests another, different way:

"If you should suffer for what is right, you are blessed. 'Do not fear what they fear; do not be frightened.' But in your hearts set apart Christ as Lord." (3:14-15)

Peter quotes in this passage the prophet Isaiah who is encouraging Israel to trust God in the face of Assyrian occupation. "Do not fear what they fear, do not be frightened." and then he encourages them to be sure to remember that Christ is Lord.

The word "Lord" is from the Greek "Kurios" and it was used in reference to those with supreme authority and power. This word was used to reference the ultimate position of kings and Caesars. And I think the fact that Peter uses that word here reminds us of the fact that we have hope for our hearts, we are not left alone defenseless.

So then, the question becomes do we trust Jesus to defend us, do we trust that God is the one who will provide for us when others insult and bring evil upon us? Or do we feel the need to retaliate, to defend ourselves? It is a question of trust.

There is something incredibly *freeing* about not having to defend yourself. We talked earlier about how Jesus, when insulted, did not retaliate but entrusted Himself to the one who judges righteously (2:23). I also think it is very *provocative* behavior.

After my dad got robbed in Mexico and had calmed down a bit from the adrenaline rush, I remember a peace coming over him. It was kind of as if it had not even happened. I think he said something to the effect, "Well, it is God's money. I guess they needed it more than we do."

My initial thought was, "You're crazy! We have been robbed and we need to do something about it!" But my father just let it go. He talked with the police I think and filed a claim when we got home, but he also seemed very much at peace.

Peter writes, "Always be prepared to give an answer to everyone who asks you to give the reason for the hope that you have," (3:16) and what I think he means is that when we repay an insult or evil with a blessing and when we recognize the authority of God on the situation, people are going to wonder what is going on. That is weird behavior, provocative.

People will start to ask questions.

This is part of the blessing we receive, I think. People look to us as something of an authority on how to handle being wronged. I do not know how many times over the years, when I feel like I have been cheated out of some money by a mechanic, the government, etc., that I have fallen back on my dad's line, "It is God's money and if He wants to spend it on a new transmission then that's His business."

It is amazing how freeing that is.

Bringing You to God *(1 Peter 3:18-22)*

Sometimes it makes sense to sacrifice a little for something bigger. This is a lesson I have been trying to teach my daughter when it comes to money. She is nine, but still the concept of saving and saying no to something now will enable her to get something she really wants down the road.

Yesterday she bought a fedora. We are going to keep trying.

My parents had a really good grasp on this. My father was a teacher and while he made a good living, they had to be careful and be smart with how they spent their money. And they also had some goals for us as a family. They loved to travel and if they were going to be able to take the six of us anywhere there were going to have to be some sacrifices.

There were several major areas in which we sacrificed: furniture, cars and school lunches.

To my knowledge, neither my mom or dad owned a new car until all of us boys had graduated from college. I think my father's philosophy was, if you start up at Point A and eventually get to Point B then you should be happy and quit griping that you have to drive your grandmother's old Plymouth Valiant that tops out at 45 mph and looks like an escapee from some 1953 sitcom.

We got this car when my dad's mother passed away. She barely drove it, maybe once a week to get groceries, so it was in good condition when Dad turned it over to the four of us. It was sea foam metallic green with probably 12-inch wheels.

It was a nice car, for a grandmother, but for a kid in high school, it was a hit to my social status, somewhere between taking your sister to prom and peeing yourself in math class (neither of which I did just to be clear). It was no Toyota Extra Cab with a Roll Bar and KC Headlights like Ronnie Matthews had, let me just put it that way.

The car itself ran fine, but it seemed to struggle with the thin air of Laramie. At just over 7,000 feet in altitude, the car had trouble breathing and would stall all the time and in the worst possible situations. We would also routinely get stuck in approximately one inch of snow, which was not only embarrassing since we were supposed to be hardy folk from the wilds of Wyoming, but highly impractical as this left only July and August that the car was operable.

But my dad never wanted to spend a lot of money on cars. He was saving for the next trip around the world. He had something bigger in mind.

The same was true with furniture. We never had anything that really matched. It probably didn't help that we had a lot of wrestling tournaments in our living room and broke quite a few couches and end tables and lamps, but I am still pretty sure my mom and dad just brought home stuff they found on the curb somewhere.

"We're just going to sit in it," my father rationalized. "Who cares what it looks like?"

Hard to argue with that kind of logic.

School lunches seemed to be another area where the Dunhams really tried to save. Most of the kids got regular baloney sandwiches with nice little slices of baloney between two slices of Wonder bread. Yum! Delicious!

I, on the other hand, got two hot dogs eviscerated and slit open lengthwise, like a high school biology experiment gone horribly wrong. My mom would usually put the ketchup on when she made the sandwich, which was nice of her and I appreciate the good intention, but by the time lunch rolled around the "sandwich" had become a light pink ball of bread dough wrapped around a bisected frankfurter.

I am pretty sure it is illegal to feed this to your kids.

The point is this: my mother and father were willing to forgo some luxuries in our daily life because they had bigger things in mind down the road. And I think this is what God has in mind when He asks us to suffer, to submit to others, to die to ourselves now; there is a reason, a payoff that we need to consider.

I think Peter explains it pretty well in this verse: "For Christ died for sins once for all, the righteous for the unrighteous, to bring you to God." (3:18)

What strikes me is the idea that Jesus' death was not for nothing; it had meaning, and that was to bring us to God. It is one thing to drive around in your grandmother's car for no reason. It is something entirely different when that car brings you a trip around the world. The car, the furniture, the weird hot dog/ketchup dough balls all make sense when you are standing at the foot of the Himalayas or under the Arc de Triomphe or gazing out over the Great Wall of China. I get to do this? Pass the dough balls, please.

Peter continues: "He was put to death in the body, but made alive by the Spirit, through whom also he went and preached to the spirits in prison who disobeyed long ago when God waited patiently in the days of Noah while the ark was being built." (3:18-20)

What?! Sometimes the Bible really takes a left turn out of nowhere, but I think what is going on here is this: Jesus dies, submits to the ridicule and suffering the Father had brought into His life, and because of that He is given a new life and thus a platform for preaching. People will listen to a guy who has been brought back to life I am pretty sure.

And so Jesus visits all the stubborn people who wouldn't get into the ark back in Noah's day, hoping, I assume, to bring them to God. Peter reminds us that not many, only eight, got into the boat and were saved. Eight out of thousands, if not tens or even hundreds of thousands of people.

It is a little unclear why Peter brings up this story at this point, but here is my take on it:

I was watching the movie *Evan Almighty* the other day and while this account of the flood has little in common with the biblical version, there was one similar theme that I could see: both Steve Carrell and Noah had to endure a boat-load (pun intended!) of ridicule and scorn and shame to build that ship.

They were constantly derided and made fun of. Their reputations were destroyed and they were dismissed as lunatics. What they were doing made absolutely no logical sense, and that, coupled with the popular opinion that they were insane, led to very low approval ratings in the polls.

It is no wonder to me that hardly anyone joined them. To join them would have meant to submit yourself to public humiliation, to disgrace. And few people can see the sense in that.

But what the people in Noah's day didn't realize was that it is through humiliation, submission, ridicule and death that one can be saved. Noah and his family endured all that because he believed God, he believed God when God said He could save them if they would just trust Him and build an ark.

I am not positively sure why Jesus went to preach to the spirits of all those people who laughed and made fun of Noah. But my hunch is that it was to give them a second chance. I know that God is patient and compassionate and wants no one to perish, (2 Peter 3:9) and it just seems like something He would do: go the extra mile in the hope of saving a few more.

And what it reminds us of is that Jesus was willing to endure the temporary pain of death for the long view of bringing us to God, like an ark through the flood waters, a baptism that "saves you by the resurrection of Jesus Christ, who has gone into heaven and is at God's right hand--with angels, authorities and powers in submission to him." (3:21-22)

The way of Jesus is not one that many take, and for a reason: it is difficult, it is full of pain and hardship and disappointment and sacrifice, like any good adventure is and should be. But it leads to an incredible place, a place that helps make sense of the journey.

JOIN THE CONVERSATION

Before you read the next chapter stop and read 1 Peter 4:1-11 and share what you think on Twitter at #Strangers&Aliens. I'd love to talk about what jumps out at you.

8 THE END IS NEAR
1 Peter 4:1-11

Most of the time I was in Nepal I stayed in our little valley. We were quite isolated, so much so that there were no roads other than the footpaths that crisscrossed through the hills and across the small farms and terraces.

About the closest thing we had to trucks were the long trains of pack horses that would come through almost daily. Thirty to forty exhausted, bone-thin animals driven by equally dirty, skinny and tired men, carried supplies and wares to remote villages and trading posts deep in the Himalayas.

They would arrive often just before dark and make camp in the small clearing behind my home. Once free from their saddles and packs, the undersized horses would roll, one after the other on the ground, stretching their backs, rubbing away the sweat and salt from the long road in the fine dust.

The men would light tiny fires if they were fortunate enough to have found some brush or sticks on the road. They would make a small pot of rice and lentils for dinner. Perhaps they might find a dry flatbread somewhere in their bags.

At night, I could hear the horses snort and move about, uncomfortable and unsure of this unfamiliar place. The men would usually talk late into the night. I could not really understand what they were saying, but I imagine most nights the talk turned to home, to family and wives and kids left behind, to whom they hoped to soon return.

They would be gone with the sun in the morning, one day closer to being home.

That may be the best part about traveling--the fact that at the end, eventually, you get to go home. I think that anyone who has traveled for a long period of time will tell you that part of what makes it fun is the understanding in the back of your mind that this trip is not going to last forever and you will be done at some point. Most people do not think about this explicitly, but on a more subconscious level.

Even though I spent most of my time in Chaur Jahari, I did have a couple of occasions to visit other hospital projects. To do this I had to fly from our valley to Nepalganj, a fairly large town on the Indian border, where I could catch what is known as the Night Bus.

The Night Bus, as its name implies, ran at night, meaning you would board the bus at around 8 p.m., drive through the night and (hopefully) arrive at your destination sometime the next morning. I am not sure exactly why they ran all these buses at night except that maybe the thinking was there is less traffic at night. Maybe they considered these "express" lines. I think that is a real stretch.

It is a little hard to explain the physical and emotional experience of the Night Bus, but I would liken it to being crammed inside a clothes dryer with an unwashed, damp bag of gym shorts and punched repeatedly in the kidneys while a strangled cat screams in your ear for about 12 hours. I am not exaggerating much.

Let me explain.

Nepali people are typically not very tall and even though their buses are usually cast-offs from India, they have been designed for people who are about six-inches shorter than myself. The main problem is that the clearance from my hip to knee cap was such that I was required to sit with my back straight, wedged in the seat.

And someone decided it would be a good idea to place a steel bar in the middle of the seat back. As the bus moved and bounced it was a little like a psychotic sixth grader kicking you from behind with steel toe boots, over and over and over.

I have ridden over some rough roads. We have some pretty gnarly tracks in Wyoming and that would have been fine in Nepal if these buses actually drove on the road. Instead, most of the trip took place in the beds of dried up rivers and streams, because, I assume, they were less rough than the regular roads.

This is a relative judgment of course. It is safe to say I have never been so violently tossed in my whole life. Even the time John Godina, the Olympic shot putter from Cheyenne, Wyoming, knocked me across John Deti field my first football game in high school felt like a pillow fight compared to this. I hit my head more than once on the ceiling of that bus and had to pardon myself about every five minutes when I would land unceremoniously in the lap of the guy sitting next to me.

I have no idea the size of the boulders we were driving over, but these were bone-jarring hits. The kind that cause your spine to crack and make you wish you had worn a mouth guard to keep your teeth from breaking in your gums.

The good news was that it was only a 12-hour trip.

Usually smells don't get to me too much. You understand that when people are struggling to feed their families, they may skip on the Old Spice Endurance at the grocers. I totally get that and I am sure I didn't smell like a daisy myself. But it is pretty amazing how sensitive the olfactory glands become when confronted with the simultaneous scent of a hundred or so weary travelers crammed in a humid, dusty tin can for a whole night.

You know how wonderful bread smells when it just comes out of the oven? This was the exact opposite of that.

The cultural influence of India on Nepal was pretty evident in the south; the further north you went it was more Tibetan and Chinese. In my opinion, one of the most distinctive elements of Indian culture has to be the music.

I suppose all eastern music has a similar tone and I am sure it is very beautiful, but for crying out loud! When played at 279 decibels for hours on end through the whole night, it can start to wear on you. I think any kind of of music, given those circumstances, would start to feel like someone is slowly ripping your brain out through your ear with tweezers. Painful.

My only explanation for the music was that it helped to keep the driver awake. A couple times though I looked to the front and it seemed like he was the only one who was sleeping. Oh well, it's the thought that counts I suppose.

I admit that I'm a little prone to hyperbole and my recollection of the actual facts may be a bit hazy, but these were brutal, exhausting trips and I honestly believe that the only thing that keep me sane was the knowledge that it would not last forever. Many times during the night I would remind myself that this would be over eventually, the words of my old shoe store boss, Gary Dodds, echoing in my ears: "You can do anything for 12 hours; you can eat a poop sandwich for 12 hours."

I am not sure he has ever ridden the Night Bus from Nepalganj to Dandledhura.

The knowledge that he will soon be home enables the traveler to endure much hardship, to push through insecurities and discomfort.

Even when the trip has been fun and enjoyable there is still a time when you are ready to go home. I can remember sitting on a grassy hill with my dad, watching the sun go down over our little hut in New Guinea. We didn't say much as we watched the shadows creep down the mountains and into our peaceful valley, something we had seen many times over the course of the year we lived there.

"Hard to believe we have been here almost a year," my father said reflectively.

"Yeah, I know."

"This has been a lot of fun."

"Yeah." Silence fell between us for a few seconds.

"I think it's time to go home," said Dad. "I think it's time."

"Yeah, me too."

It's always fun and exciting to go somewhere new, but it's even better, after a long trip, to go home. In fact, I think that the knowledge we would be going home, maybe a week or a month or a year later, made most of our trips bearable. It is amazing to me how the reality that "we won't be here forever" changes your attitude and energizes your spirit.

And I don't think this is really a reflection on any one place. I can remember being in some of the most quaint and interesting little towns in Europe and thinking, "Man, I just want to go home!" It is not the fact that some place is bad or awful, it is just that there is only one place we can call home. And that is what our heart longs and yearns for.

The Rest of Your Earthly Life *(1 Peter 4:1-2)*

For some reason, when you realize that time is limited and this life does not go on forever, it makes it a lot easier to put up with hardship and to say no to temptation. You just gut things out more.

When I ran track I always liked the shorter races better. Both the five-mile and the half-mile were hard, but the half-mile lasted less than 2 minutes, which by my calculations is way better than around 25 minutes for the five-mile race. I think the sooner you see the finish line the stronger your will becomes. It is easier to fall apart if you think a race will never end.

And I think a lot of it has to do with pain. Most of us are averse to pain (with good reason! It hurts!) which can be a good thing. Pain is the body's way of protecting itself from further damage.

But sometimes it is necessary and important to push through pain. Pain forms character. Pain makes us stronger. Sometimes doing the right thing is painful. Unfortunately, many times it just seems easier to give in and do what we know is not the right thing, but at the moment it is the less painful option.

When I was in college I found myself on the cross country team my sophomore year. I had played football my freshman year, but decided to switch for a couple of reasons. First, I wasn't getting to play as much as I thought I would on the football team and, second, cross country took up a lot less time. For practice you just showed up, ran around for an hour, went home. No big deal.

With football, you had super long and boring practices where you spent most of your time standing around as the coaches tried to explain how much tougher players were in their day or the intricacies and poetic beauty of the single wing offense. (Note: We were the only college in America still running the single wing at the time, probably because it was the most ridiculous offense on the planet. No quarterback! Just hike it to the fullback and off you go!)

Cross country just seemed like a better use of my time. I probably should have done a little more research.

The thing I didn't entirely realize is that five miles is a really long time to have to run as fast as you can. And running as fast as you can for that distance is quite painful, both physically and mentally.

Actually the mental pain is probably the hardest part of the whole thing. You have these inner monologues going on telling you how much your body is hurting and how dumb you were for ever leaving football and how you could be sipping Gatorade right now and pounding your head against a 300-pound defensive tackle and wouldn't that feel so much better?

My cross country coach in college was a farmer named Phil Torrens. He stood about 5'6" and had a huge grey mustache. His skin was brown and leathery from years on his tractor growing corn up in Utica.

I have no idea how a farmer becomes a college track and cross-country coach, but he put his heart and soul into our team and he gave some pretty inspirational speeches before our races.

Coach Torrens knew that there was going to be a time during that race, a moment when each of us would decide if we were going to push through the pain and finish strong, or if we were going to, in essence, give up and jog on home.

Coach usually got pretty emotional at this point of the speech. His eyes would narrow and he would look at each of us as if trying to peer into our souls.

"Gentlemen, (he always called us gentlemen, which I thought was nice) gentlemen, today you have before you an opportunity, an opportunity to do something special..." Actually, we had the same opportunity every week, but we didn't interrupt him.

"Today, you can go out there and give it your best. You have the opportunity to come together as a team and to overcome adversity and win this race!" At this point he'd usually throw in a couple expletives about how he hated a certain team or coach, typically our rival, Ohio Wesleyan.

"There is going to come a time in this race when you will have to decide if you are going to finish the race or not! Finish the race, gentlemen, finish the race!"

William Wallace he was not, but we all appreciated that he wanted us to do well, to not have any regrets at the end of the day. That's what happens when you quit during a race. You regret that you didn't push through to the end.

Probably my only regret as a collegiate athlete happened when I basically gave up at our conference championship my senior year. It is embarrassing to even talk about. I don't remember the course, but I do recall that the ground was covered in snow and quite slick.

Our team was the three-time defending champions and we were expected to win again. This was my third year of running, so I was picked to finish in the top ten; I thought I could go top five no problem.

The race started fast, about 4:45 for the first mile. There was a lot of pushing, but these were a bunch of 125-pound nerds, so that didn't bother me too much.

I'd say it was about three miles in that I started to feel the wall of pain emerge. It is hard to describe exactly what it feels like, but basically what happens is that your legs literally start to fill up with poison, lactic acid generated from a deficiency of oxygen in your blood.

It is a gradual hurt, maybe like you are slowly being crushed by one of those giant steamrollers they use to level out roads and highways.

When the pain starts to creep in, it becomes a real mental game, trying to convince yourself that you feel great, that you are light as a feather and fast when you actually feel like someone just strapped a piano to your back.

The moment of decision had come. Coach Torrens' sparkling blue eyes flashed before me. I tried to relax my aching muscles and visualize passing other runners who seem much fresher than me. I pictured the finish line approaching quickly.

And then it happened. I hit a patch of snow on the side of a hill and my feet went out from under me. I slid about seven or eight feet before coming to a stop. Someone's spikes grazed my shoulder as they tried to avoid the carnage.

This was the only time in my cross-country career that I fell, and it did me in. It is amazing how much physical effort it takes to get back up and going again. It takes even more effort mentally.

And I am ashamed to say I didn't have it in me on that day. I distinctly remember thinking, "I'm done."

The rest of the race was a blur. I remember being passed by quite a few people. I just couldn't get going again. I think I ended up around 30th. Our team lost by only a few points. It is one of the great disappointments of my life. I know I quit on my team, my coach and myself.

The race was only 25 minutes long and maybe that is why I still think about it today, over twenty years later. I could have kept going, it was only a half hour of pain.

Peter really wants us to keep going. To not give up or give in.

"Therefore, since Christ suffered in his body, arm yourselves also with the same attitude, because he who has suffered in his body is done with sin. As a result, he does not live the rest of his earthly life for evil human desires, but rather for the will of God."

I know for me some days it feels like my earthly life will never end, that I will have to struggle forever against sin. And many days I lose the battle, I give up, give in to anger and selfishness. I quit leading a life where I care more about others than myself, where I let others win and take advantage of me. I push back and refuse to submit to others any more because submission hurts and is not really all that much fun.

In some way it is comforting to know that Jesus suffered when He was a man on earth. And it encourages me to know that He didn't give up. He pressed on. I don't always do that, but He makes me want to.

Enough Time *(1 Peter 4:3-6)*

I don't think I have a ton of bad habits, but there are things that I tend to do often that I acknowledge might be a bit outside of normal.

For example, I like to eat cereal in the shower. Most people think this is weird. I do my best to explain that you don't hold the bowl under the water. I am not taking a shower *with* my cereal, I am simply eating cereal while *in* the shower. I love the warmth of the water on my back and the cool sweet food in my throat. It is a lovely combination. You should try it. I promise the first time won't be your last.

I have other habits I am trying to form. I try to run and get some exercise on a regular basis. I am working to eat better foods. And I am trying to spend time in my Bible and write a little everyday.

And then I have habits that just seemed to emerge on their own.

I have to admit that I was a little behind the times when it came to Facebook. I feel sufficiently caught up now, but it took me a maybe a year longer than most to get plugged in to the social network.

It is safe to say that it has become a habit for me. I have the Facebook app on my phone and I scroll through the newsfeed at least a couple of times a day. I am not a huge contributor to the culture in that I do not often post or update my status or play farm games, but I do enjoy seeing what others are up to. I just realized that probably makes me some kind of stalker, or is it a voyeur?

In any case, it has somehow gotten into my routine to check my newsfeed when I first get up in the morning and periodically throughout the day. Sometimes there are dozens if not a hundred updates to browse, and not that you all are not interesting, but sometimes I think I really have better things I should be spending my time on.

And I'm guessing I'm not alone in that sentiment. This morning, in fact, I read this update from a girl I went to high school with:

"UNPLUGGING FROM FACEBOOK FOR AWHILE. I HAVE 2 AMAZING, WONDERFUL, ADORABLE CHILDREN WHO I DON'T GET ENOUGH TIME WITH AS IT IS AND I SPEND TOO MUCH DAMN TIME ON HERE, SO THAT TIME IS NOW GOING TO MY CHILDREN."

I had to laugh a bit, because I see this kind of update probably on a weekly basis. People just coming to the conclusion that they have spent more than enough time on Facebook and it is time to move on. I assume by the ALL CAPS that this time she is serious!

This is by no means a judgment against Facebook, which I think is a great way to connect and reconnect with people in your life. The reality is that sometimes we get sucked into habits without realizing it, and sometimes a switch goes off in our heads where we begin to ask, "What in the world am I doing? I just wasted an hour!"

When it comes to how we are living our lives I think there is undoubtedly a tension between the way God wants us to live and the way things typically go down in the world around us.

Peter has constantly been encouraging us to submit, to put others before ourselves, to love, to be compassionate and humble, to bless those who do evil and insult us. Without a doubt he is suggesting that this is a better way to live and we should strongly consider it.

I think Peter understands that because we are sojourners, travelers in a foreign land, we are going to get swept up from time to time in the way things are done here. It is to be expected. In fact, before we know Christ, before we become a part of His kingdom and bear His name, it is all we know.

Living in a foreign land you are going to try some of the local customs, traditions and ways of doing things. In Nepal, I ate a lot of rice and lentils. And chai made with buffalo milk, which is very good and has some unusual, but interesting spices. Sometimes this was my fare for every meal in a day. And I could live with that, to a point.

Eventually, there comes a point when you think, "OK, I have done the Nepali thing, let's get some eggs and bacon and toast for this American kid. Enough is enough."

I think Peter wants us to move on, too. Enough is enough. "You have spent enough time in the past doing what pagans choose to do–living in debauchery, lust, drunkenness, orgies, carousing and detestable idolatry…[it is time to] live according to God in regard to the spirit." (4:3, 6)

This past winter I had to get a physical for some life insurance. Part of the process is that the insurance company sends a nurse to your office to check your blood pressure, measure your height and weight, ask you a few questions and draw some blood.

For the most part I consider myself a healthy person. I try to eat right and get a little exercise when I can. I am no triathlete anymore by any stretch, but I am not a couch potato either. At least I didn't think so, until I stepped on the scale. I am not going to even tell you how much I weighed, but the nurse said to me, (I'm not kidding!) "Well, it is the holidays, you know."

I had been feeling like I could use lose a few, but the scale told me I needed to quit goofing off and I better lose about 25 lbs.

Physical health is important. Spiritual health even more so.

"You have spent enough time in the past doing what pagans choose to do-- living in debauchery, lust, drunkenness, orgies, carousing and detestable idolatry. They think it strange that you do not plunge with them into the same flood of dissipation, and they heap abuse on you." (4:3-4)

I got serious about my walk with God the year we lived in Budapest, Hungary, the year my dad was on sabbatical leave from the University of Wyoming. The next year I went college in Ohio and really dug into my faith.

When I went home for Christmas that year, I met up with a few old high school friends a very different person from the one who left a couple years earlier. I know that it was really hard for them to understand why I was no longer interested in the same kind of activities and recreation as when we were teenagers.

I tried to explain that I was trying to follow God and those things just no longer held any appeal. They were good friends, but I know it didn't make a lot of sense to them. I never felt judged by them and they didn't "heap abuse" on me that I know of. But we did start to drift apart.

That was a sad time for me in many ways, but I also knew that this was a new direction for me. I had spent enough time in that world. I was happy to move on, to discover what lay ahead.

The End of All Things Is Near *(1 Peter 4:7-11)*

One of the hardest times to concentrate and be diligent with a task is when things are winding down to a conclusion. It is difficult at times to finish well.

Right now I have a bathroom with an unfinished floor and a shower control knob in pieces in the tub. There has been very little movement to get this fixed in the past week, and I am not really aware of any development plan in place at the moment. I have to shower downstairs.

I am pretty sure I am not the only one who struggles with finishing things. I live about an hour south of Pittsburgh and travel from time to time on Interstate 79. The Pennsylvania Department of Transportation has been continuously working on the 45-mile stretch of road between Morgantown and Washington, PA for literally 15 years. I doubt they will ever finish.

(On a side note, the irony that it is taking me a really long time to finish this chapter is not lost on me either.)

We need a reminder from time to time, that, well, time is running out. Things are not always going to be as they are. The clock is ticking; get to work.

My father had a way of motivating me and my brothers to eat when I was a young boy. He would set the timer on the stove, and if our plates weren't clear when the timer rang, it was off to bed. The genius of it (or what I would call the evil genius) was that you got your plate back in the morning for breakfast.

Brussel sprouts are horrible, nasty, little vegetables from the garden of Satan himself, but they are even worse cold at 7 a.m. while everyone around you is enjoying fresh French toast with warm syrup and crispy bacon.

You didn't let the food timer run out too many times.

I think Peter understands this tendency in us. He writes, "The end of all things is near. Therefore be clear minded and self-controlled so that you can pray. Above all, love each other deeply…." (4:7-8)

I think ol' Pete was a pretty simple guy and I like that he doesn't get too complex with his theology. Because the end is near, we need to do two things: one, spend time with God and, two, spend time with people.

In the first case, we need to pray. Talking is probably the primary way we connect with anyone and prayer is the primary means God has given us to connect with Him, to share our lives with our Father.

Secondly, Peter encourages us, in light of the end being near, to be about people and to leverage our gifts, abilities, resources to that end. I have never been a big talker or one to share my "feelings," but I love more than anything to sit and talk with my nine-year old daughter, to hear about her day, to listen to what is on her mind.

116

I know she is not always going to live with me so I try to soak up those opportunities to talk with her as much as I can.

Of course, sometimes basketball is on and that just is a whole lot more interesting to me than a discussion about Monster High dolls. I am working on being a better dad.

"Each one should use whatever gift he has received to serve others, faithfully administering God's grace in its various forms. If anyone speaks, he should do it as one speaking the very words of God. If anyone serves, he should do it with all the strength God provides, so that in all things God may be praised through Jesus Christ." (4:10-11)

It makes sense that we need God to empower us to finish well, and that at the end of the day, He gets the credit. Whatever we say, however we serve, and what we do should be an outpouring of God's love for people.

What I find a little funny is the fact that Peter brings up what I think is a pretty specific scenario when talking about perseverance. He writes, "Offer hospitality to one another without grumbling." (4:9)

I think most of us have had guests to our house from time to time. Maybe a friend or relative has come for a night or two, or in some extreme cases, a week or two. Anyone who has had this experience of trying to be hospitable probably appreciates Peter's encouragement, "The end of all things is near."

Over the past five or six years, my home has become something of a haven for directionless, impoverished, down-on-their-luck guys.

To be fair, I offered both room and board to each of them, as a manifestation of the goodness and purity of my heart. And in every case I have wondered what in the world I was thinking.

There is a good chance that Corey, Ryan and Addison (yeah, he's a dude) will be reading this, so let me just say, it's not you, it's me.

To be honest they were all really good roommates: considerate, tidy, respectful and helpful with things around the house. They just happened to share a house with a cantankerous old man who is pretty set in his ways.

I have realized through the years that I like to be alone, or maybe I should say, I am no longer in college and I do not prefer to have roommates. I think that happens as we get older, more toward the end of life. We get set in our ways, people annoy us more. It becomes, on some level, more difficult to endure others and to be hospitable.

Not by any means am I saying that this is acceptable or the right thing to do, and if anything I think Peter is encouraging us to up the ante on hospitality; spend *more* time, not less, with people as we near the end.

This past week I took my daughter, Grace, to New York City. Several times as we walked through Central Park, or rode on the subway, or sat in a restaurant, it occurred to me how quickly she is growing up. It is cliché, I know. But I feel like, in some ways, the end is near. Not in a literal, death-sense, but more that she is changing and these days I have with her are growing few.

At the end of the day, when everything else passes and fades, two things really matter: spend time with God because He matters; pray. And spend time with the people God has in your life; be hospitable.

JOIN THE CONVERSATION

Before you read the next chapter stop and read 1 Peter 4:12-19 and share what you think on Twitter at #Strangers&Aliens. I'd love to talk about what jumps out at you.

9 BEARING THE NAME
1 Peter 4:12-19

Depending on where you go, being an American can mean different things. Rightly or wrongly, in some parts of the world it makes you a rock star; in others it makes you the scum of the earth. It doesn't always happen, but for some reason you will from time to time get judged based on your nationality.

Thankfully, I have probably experienced it more in a positive manner than negative. By and large, Americans have favorable support around the world.

When I was in graduate school I got hooked up with a group of guys involved in a campus ministry band. I had learned to play a little guitar a few years earlier and they were pretty desperate for a rhythm guitar, so I got the job. It was a lot of fun. We played for the weekly meeting and enjoyed a little notoriety as the house band, but more than anything we were all good friends.

Second semester, one of the guys got the idea that we should take our band on the road. He had a missionary contact in Bulgaria, Andy, who wanted to line up a few gigs for us in the college town where he was trying to get a Christian group going. The idea was that we would be the cool American band that would give Andy the attention and leverage he needed for his ministry.

It is important to note that at that time Bulgaria was just coming out of decades of isolation from the influence of communism. Their people had long been "protected" from Western culture, but now the flood gates were opening all over Eastern Europe and they simply could not get enough of the West, especially popular culture.

Andy figured this was the perfect time to cash in and we couldn't have agreed more.

And so Pascal's Wager was born, rehearsals began, tickets were purchased, gigs booked and promotional posters with our cool, rock-star visages announcing our imminent arrival were soon plastered all over Bucharest. It wasn't quite like the Beatles coming to America, but I'd say it was close.

Our band was called Pascal's Wager after the famous French mathematician, physicist and philosopher, Blaise Pascal. He had formulated a famous argument for becoming a Christian that is known as Pascal's Wager, which basically says you have nothing to lose in becoming Christian, but everything to gain. Conversely, you have everything to lose by rejecting it and not so much to gain. The smart money, Pascal argued, is on Jesus.

We also chose this name because a random guy walking by a rehearsal one night heard our awesome jams and asked if he could sit in and listen. We were like, "Rock on! Of course you can!" As it turns out, his name was Pascal.

The plan was to spend spring break in Bulgaria. Andy had lined up gigs at local bars and pubs and college student hangouts each night. One night we were to play in the Bulgarian national concert hall, which we thought made us a pretty big deal.

Apparently our Bulgarian publicity team thought we were a pretty big deal as well. When we arrived in Bucharest, we found out that our posters claimed we were the second best band in Virginia. I am not sure where they got that information, but it was horribly erroneous on many levels, and on behalf of Pascal's Wager, I want to offer a sincere apology to any and all bands, past or present, from Virginia.

First of all, we were not from Virginia. West Virginia is its own state, but in the Bulgarians' defense, most people from America don't realize that either. Ask any West Virginian and they will tell you that when you say "I'm from West Virginia," someone will invariably reply, "Oh, yeah, I've got an aunt in Richmond." Anyway, more importantly, I think it is pretty safe to say we were not the second best band from anywhere. We were pretty terrible I am sure.

I will say this: we had some really talented people, really good musicians in the band. We just didn't have the time to come together as a musical unit.

But sometimes how good you are doesn't really matter. It's all about the novelty of the show, and for us the real draw was the fact that we were from America. And apparently there were plenty of people interested in hearing what a bunch of kids from the USA could bring.

We played five or six shows and I was shocked at how many people turned out. Maybe it is just the years that have added to the numbers, but people seemed to be really interested and excited about us. We had a couple shows with more than a few hundred people there.

I even remember being interviewed by Bulgarian television after a gig at the National Puppet Theater. (I know, I had never heard of such a thing either.) Apparently they filmed us and planned to use the footage on their version of MTV. Again, let me apologize to all the people of Bulgaria. I am pretty sure it was that show that our lead singer, Luke, fashioned a puppet out of someone's sock. The two of them did a couple of duets, if I remember correctly.

Maybe people did come out to see us because we were Americans and that was new and novel, but I think the veil was lifted pretty quickly for them once the show began.

We were just a garage band from west of Virginia; pretty average stuff.

Actually it was a very humbling experience. Often after a show, people would come up to talk with us and ask to play our guitars or drums or whatever. Without fail they would start laying down licks like Jimi Hendrix himself. We would try to remain as cool as possible and say things like, "Yeah man, that's awesome. Keep practicing."

Inside we were thinking, *this* guy should be on Bulgarian MTV, not us goofballs!

I have to believe that on some level we were a disappointment. There are a lot of great American bands out there and I just don't think we were one of them. Maybe that is what those Bulgarians were hoping for. We bore the weight of expectation.

Fortunately, they loved America and therefore they loved us, at least that is what it seemed like to us and we were very thankful for that.

Often, though, there can be real tension between cultures. Given all the wars and conflicts we have going on, that may be about the most obvious statement anyone could ever make, but the point is that tension and conflict is unfortunately more the norm than what we experienced in Bulgaria. Cultures clash. Tensions rise. Misunderstandings abound. This is not abnormal. And sometimes it is good to remind ourselves that this is the case.

I think Peter wants to encourage and remind us that we should not be surprised when trials and suffering come to us, that this is part of what it means to carry the name "Christian" and that when things get rough, when we suffer for doing good, we should not give up.

Something Strange Happening to You *(1 Peter 4:12-13)*

"Dear friends, do not be surprised at the painful trial you are suffering, as though something strange were happening to you. But rejoice that you participate in the sufferings of Christ, so that you may be overjoyed when his glory is revealed" (4:12-13).

To be honest, I have no idea what a life where suffering is the *norm* is like. For me, suffering and pain are an aberration, an abnormality. I know there are people all over the world who suffer tremendously and on a regular basis for their faith. I'm just not one of them.

And so I have to say it does come as a bit of a surprise when I suffer a bit.

Most commentators don't seem to know exactly what Peter was referring to when he wrote these words, but some speculate that he was talking about the impending destruction of the temple in Jerusalem.

The temple was the center of Jewish life and culture. In many ways it defined them as a people. And for a group that saw their connection with God and the temple as one in the same, the psychological damage must have been tremendous when it was destroyed by the Romans.

But I think Peter may have been talking about something else. These new Christians had, in many ways, abandoned the temple in Jerusalem.

122

They had a new understanding of God and that God was living within them now through the Holy Spirit. They no longer had a need for a physical temple.

Some translations call it a "fiery" trial. I wonder if Peter wasn't referring to Nero's use of Christians as human torches. I think Peter is probably right to say that we shouldn't be surprised by trials, but come on! Human torches? That's nuts! And absolutely horrible.

I guess I just figure if someone ever abuses me it is far more likely that it is because I deserve it than because I am a Christian. I think if I actually went through some kind of persecution for my faith I would be more than surprised. I'd be shocked.

When I started grad school, I had exactly forty-three dollars in my bank account. From what I hear, that's sort of a common denominator among people who decide to go to grad school. Few people who have nice paying jobs and a house in the suburbs say, "I think I'll leave all this and go to graduate school." No, this is often a decision made by people with no money.

Fortunately, I was able to land a spot as an RA, a resident advisor in one of the dorms. I wasn't super thrilled about living in the dorms again, but I was pretty stoked to get a tuition waiver, a meal plan, a room with a bed and a monthly stipend. Freshman puking in the elevator at 2 a.m.? Sign me up!

Actually I really loved that first year. They assigned me the foreign exchange student floor, so for one thing all the kids were older, and although they liked to party, they were a bit more mature about it.

I also fell in with a great group of Christians. They were quite tolerant of me and the fact that I had not used deodorant in well over a year. You kind of forget about those kind of social niceties having just come from rural Nepal.

I have never been particularly shy about my faith, and at that time I was especially cognizant that God had done a lot of work in my life. I thought faith and spirituality were interesting subjects to talk about, and I was very appreciative that a few peers had challenged my way of thinking about God several years before. Those conversations had stirred a spiritual awakening in me. I am glad those college students weren't too timid to get those conversations going.

My point is that talking about God and my faith was (and is) a pretty natural part of how I am, so it made sense for me to want to engage people in spiritual conversations wherever I lived. And at this time I happened to live in the dorms.

I remember one afternoon stopping by a kid's room. He was writing a paper, but had his door wide open which usually meant something like, "Please come in and save me from this horrible thing I have to do."

His name was Zach and we had met several times in the dining hall, around the dorm, etc. We weren't best friends by any means, but we knew each other, so I stepped into the room and asked what he was up to.

We had talked a few times before about spiritual things and so I directed the conversation that way again. I don't recall that we got too deep into it; a few thoughts back and forth about Jesus and the resurrection, the afterlife, and that was about it.

I said my goodbyes and left his room, not really thinking much of it.

Two days later that all changed.

In my mailbox I received a letter from the university's Office of Social Justice. It informed me that a complaint had been filed by the student president of the campus student Jewish organization. I was a little confused until I realized that this had been done on Zach's behalf. Apparently he told someone about our conversation and this got the ball rolling.

It is hard to be objective about these things. I honestly don't remember being pushy or confrontational, and if I was then I deserved being reprimanded.

But I think this was more personal. I think this was mostly about a guy who didn't like Christians and saw a chance to get one in trouble.

The Office of Social Justice was run by a lady named Melissa Something-or-Other and she requested a meeting. I remember going into her office and sitting down across from her. A huge desk sat between us.

"You can't talk to students about their faith."

"Why not, isn't this a university where we talk about ideas?"

"Yes, but you are an RA and students see you as an authority figure. You have an undue amount of influence over them. They feel pressure to do what you tell them."

Apparently this lady had never been an RA in a freshman dorm. In no way, shape or form did I ever meet a kid who felt the authoritarian position of an RA was influential enough to turn down their stereo, much less convert to another religion.

I don't remember exactly what happened, but I got reprimanded by the university and was blackballed by the resident faculty leaders that oversaw our dorm. They refused to renew my contract for the following school year. Fortunately, I got picked up off waivers by another dorm.

Peter says to rejoice when we face trials because we get to share in the suffering of Christ, and because we share in His suffering we will be all that more excited when we get to see Jesus glorified and people appreciate and applaud Him as he should be appreciated and applauded.

I have never been beaten. Never been flogged. Never really been mocked or abused for my faith. But I do feel like I was singled out for my faith. I feel like I could have talked freely about Islam or Hinduism or just about anything except Jesus. For some reason that guy really ticks people off.

There is something good about pain, something wonderful about suffering. For me the best part about it is when it is over. I used to love being done with a really hard race. Crossing the finish line, exhausted, muscles aching. It feels so good to be able to stop.

The other thing I love about suffering is that, once it is over, you get to talk about it. You get to share stories. And this is especially fun to do with people who have been through the same kind of suffering.

I love to sit around with my brothers and recount the hardships and trials we have had traveling. My brother Tim and I are getting ready to go visit our brother Jon in Brazil this week. I am pretty sure we are going to spend time telling stories about different trials and adventures we have been through.

Tim and I would drive that old Volkswagen bus home from college in Ohio to Wyoming each Christmas. It was a long trip, 24-hours non stop, through about -400 degree weather in Iowa and Nebraska. The bad part about it was that VW buses have literally no heat. We had to wear snow boots and parkas and cover ourselves with blankets to keep from freezing to death.

We actually carried a scraper to remove ice from the *inside* of the windshield.

Miserable cold, but one of our favorite stories and one that I tell often. That story and hundreds of others bind me and my brothers together. I know we had some easy and fun times, too, but we are tied together through pain and suffering.

I think when we get to heaven we will get to tell those stories, and I think Jesus will be there and He will ask us to tell the story of the time we suffered for Him, the time we got hurt, but we hung in there and kept pressing on.

And we will be glad and proud that we did, because when Jesus tells His story and shares with us how hard it was and how much it hurt, we will feel like we were part of it, like we were there in a way.

The Family of Suffering *(1 Peter 4:14-18)*

I think we get it from my father, but people in my family take a certain pride in being different. My younger brother Jon is currently in Brazil. For the last 10 years or so he has been walking to Patagonia with his donkey. A few weeks ago he emailed me and told me that he was at a rodeo and the organizers made him lead his donkey around the arena while everyone gawked and the announcer talked about him.

He said it was ridiculous, but let's be honest, his life is kind of ridiculous. I couldn't even begin to tell you how many people, after hearing his story, have said, "That is so cool." Most people have no idea how hard it is to travel, to constantly be on the road, not knowing where your next meal is going to be or where you will sleep that night.

But people are fascinated by the unusual. Jon has become quite the celebrity in South America. He claims it is because of his donkey, Whothey, but he gets *tons* of press inquiries and has been on major television programs and newspapers in pretty much every country from Mexico to Brazil. He even made the *New York Times* a few years ago.

One of the shows featuring Jon had to be the Venezuelan version of Entertainment Tonight. The video starts out with a super-fancy professional graphics package after which a high-angle camera sweeps in on a beautiful "news" anchor in a spotless, modern studio. She is wearing a miniskirt and four-inch stiletto heels, long brown hair to her waist.

She is speaking Spanish, but I gather that she is very excited about this next story, a story of friendship and adventure, a story of hardship and trial, the story of a man and his burro.

The camera cuts to the field reporter who is standing on the edge of a field, next to a busy highway. He has a huge moustache and slicked back brown hair. He looks soulfully into the camera as speeding trucks scream by, narrowly missing taking him out.

He gives his opening monologue about this young traveler, how he has come to their country from America with his trusty burro. As he slowly walks along the highway, microphone in hand, he recounts Jon's long journey from Mexico, through Central America, how he boarded a boat in Panama to avoid the dangerous regions of northern Columbia only to be ambushed by pirates off the coast of Venezuela (true story).

"And now," the presenter continues, "this American has made his way to our country..." and the camera pulls back to reveal my brother, dressed something like a hobo, something of a sheepish grin on his mug, gently stroking Whothey's long, scruffy head.

As his brother I find it pretty hilarious that the media in South America find him so interesting, but if I put myself in their shoes it makes a little sense. Most people just do not know what to do with this blond-haired, blue-eyed American walking through their town with a donkey. It defies explanation on many levels and that is pretty fascinating.

But what is equally interesting is the fact that people react in many different ways to Jon. In some places he has been welcomed, in others ignored, tolerated in some, robbed, abused, cared for, made fun of, made a celebrity. It has run the gamut.

I wonder, sometimes, why some people open their homes to Jon and others ignore him, why some share what they have and others try to steal from him. It is a really curious thing to me.

On one level we cannot really control how people view us, the judgments they make. People are going to form their own opinions regardless of the facts. And who knows what motivates them. Perhaps they have pre-formed notions, good or bad, about the United States, about Americans, and their minds made up before even getting to know Jon.

Peter reminds us that sometimes we are going to suffer just because we are Christians, just because of the name we bear. I am guessing what he means is that people are going to look down on you, maybe form certain opinions, because they find out you go to church or that Jesus is important to you.

When you become a Christian, you buy into a different way of life, a new way of seeing the world and people and vocation and everything. And it should be no surprise that this is going to rub people the wrong way from time to time. People are testy about things unfamiliar.

Peter says that if you are insulted "because of the name of Christ" (4:14) you are blessed. Which I take to mean, people just know this thing about you, that you are a Christian, and they choose to beat you down based on that fact alone. Kind of like they dismiss Jon because he is different or from another country.

This is a good kind of rejection. An insult that leads to blessing.

However, Peter doesn't want us to get this kind of suffering to get confused with the fact that sometimes we suffer because we are jerks.

"If you suffer, it should not be as a murderer or a thief or any other kind of criminal, or even as a meddler. However, if you suffer as a Christian, do not be ashamed, but praise God that you bear that name." (4:15-16)

I have known a few people over the years who have told me that they were being persecuted at work or in school because of their faith, and I have seriously had the thought, "I think you're being persecuted because you're a boob. "

I think Peter is reminding us to ask the question, why am I running into people? Why am I having conflict? Is it because we fundamentally see the world in a different way or is it because I am just hard to get along with?

It is a good question to ask.

We are all going to have critics, people who don't like us or have formed negative opinions. I guess what Peter is saying is that if you are going to have people not like you, don't let it be for a really good reason, let it be for something shallow. Let them not like you because of your name.

Continuing *(1 Peter 4:19)*

I love that Peter is constantly reminding us that we are on a hard road, we have a hard life if we live in the submissive way God has laid out for His people. And I love that one of the central messages Peter keeps hammering is "don't give up." He writes, "So then, those who suffer according to God's will should commit themselves to their faithful Creator and *continue* to do good." (4:19, emphasis added).

The *New American Standard* translation offers a little different slant: "Therefore, those also who suffer according to the will of God shall entrust their souls to a faithful Creator in doing what is right."

The word "entrust" is interesting in the Greek because it carries the sense of setting a table of food out for someone. This word is used in pretty much all the accounts where Jesus miraculously provides bread and fish for thousands of hungry people.

There is probably not a more basic or daily need than food. Well, maybe air and perhaps water, but you get the point. We need to eat it every day, day after day; it never really ends.

I wonder sometimes, if God ever gets tired of the monotony of feeding us. Almost every morning I make my daughter's lunch for school. I am not very creative so she usually gets an assortment of deli meats and crackers, fruit, vegetable, water and some sort of cookie or other sweet treat. On other days it's a peanut butter sandwich via tortilla, fruit, vegetable, water and some sort of cookie or other sweet treat.

If I am completely honest, there are days I'd rather not make her lunch. It just gets old. (I know what you're thinking, but for some reason the option of school lunch never seems to cross my mind at that hour of the day.) Don't get me wrong, I love the *idea* of providing a good healthy meal for my child, it is just the actual *providing* that I grow tired of sometimes.

Of course I realize I am a terrible father and no one else has those urges to tell their kids to go make their own lunch for once, but my point is that

God is a good Father and He never tires, day after day, of setting a good meal before us, providing, doing good for those He loves.

Truth be told, I am always going to feed my daughter. Giving up on that is just kind of out of the question.

We had an open campus in high school, which basically just meant you could leave school to go to lunch instead of having to eat in the cafeteria. My friends and I could go anywhere we wanted, but for some reason we ended up at our house a lot.

The Dunhams lived about two miles or so from the high school, and so every day we would sprint to Reagan and haul butt over to Barrett Street to eat.

I can only imagine we must have burst through that front door like a bunch of ravenous dogs, which probably explains why my mom always had a ton of food ready to go on the table. She probably was worried she might get eaten otherwise.

On a typical school day there would be four to five guys there. We would eat a loaf of bread's-worth of sandwiches, a gallon of milk, a bag of chips, a few dozen cookies. Vegetables were a waste of time though, so Mom quit putting those out after a few half-hearted protestations that we needed to eat *something* healthy.

It must have looked something like a piranha feeding frenzy, bits of lunch meat and cheese flying through the air as we scarfed down everything in site.

And then we were gone. Like a swarm of locusts, we disappeared with a few guttural "Thank you, Mom/Mrs. Dunham"-s tossed back over our shoulders.

Not once did I ever think what this experience must have been like for my mother. And it was not just me. I was there with my friends, but it was also Tim and Jon and Joe with their friends. She probably made close to ten thousand lunches for boys in that high school over the years.

And this happened every day. For years. And she never complained, never really mentioned it. She just kept on buying bread and milk, making cookies and sandwiches. Pretty unreal.

I am sure there were days she didn't really feel like making lunch for a dozen animals, but I guess there are certain things that you can't really quit. And family is one of them.

In all honesty, what other option do we have? I lost count a long time ago the times I was ready to quit being a Dunham. My family is a bunch of maniacs! But what could I do? This is who I am and so I keep plugging along. Day after day after day, being the best Dunham I can be.

One of my favorite passages is a story about when a bunch of people were leaving Jesus because He was starting to say some freaky, challenging stuff. He turned to His own disciples and asked, "Are you going to leave me, too?"

I think maybe they looked around at each other for a minute before Peter finally spoke up, "Lord, to whom shall we go? You have the words of eternal life." (John 6:68) Absolutely brilliant. Where else are we going to go? And so we continue to live, best we can, the life laid out for us, because we bear the name of Christ.

It is boring sometimes, it is daily, it is challenging, but we keep moving, keep serving, keep submitting, keep setting out a plate.

JOIN THE CONVERSATION

Before you read the next chapter stop and read 1 Peter 5:1-11 and share what you think on Twitter at #Strangers&Aliens. I'd love to talk about what jumps out at you.

10 BROTHERS THROUGHOUT THE WORLD
1 Peter 5:1-11

Because my father was a physical education teacher (well, technically a professor at a university, but when convenient we liked to remind him he was just a glorified gym teacher) and I grew up with three brothers, it makes sense that we played a lot of sports and were on a lot of teams. Growing up we played football, baseball, basketball, soccer, ran track, and wrestled. From grade school through college, there was rarely a time we weren't on a team of some sort.

Say what you will about sports producing self-involved, egomaniacal humans, it also has a way of uniting people.

I think this is for a couple of reasons: one, you spend an awful lot of time with your teammates. Good or bad they kind of become your surrogate family. As I mentioned, during high school our football coaches took us for eight or nine days to Guernsey, Wyoming where we saw no one except the 80 or 90 other guys on the team. During the season, we had practice for three hours every day after school. Factor that in with traveling for sometimes up to eight hours one-way for a game, and I spent more time with those knuckleheads than I did my own family. Bonds are created.

Second, I think adversity draws you together. People in sports face at least two kinds of adversity. The physical and mental toll some sports can take is tremendous. I wrestled one spring in eighth grade. You don't know pain until some guy tries to tear your arm off at the same time your face is crammed into his armpit. I decided that sport was not for me. But the point is that everyone on the team is experiencing that pain together, and that somehow unites you, brings you together.

The second unifying aspect of adversity athletes experience is that of a shared opponent/enemy. In high school our rival was Cheyenne Central. I have no idea why we hated them so much other than the fact that they were the closest school to us, so I guess by default became our rival.

I didn't particularly hate Cheyenne Central. Didn't know them. They had never done anything rude or unbecoming that I was aware of. Well, I guess I did tell you I got flattened by John Godina my first play in a varsity game, but I felt that was all well within the rules and bounds of the game. Nothing to be bitter about there.

Our coach, John Deti, now he hated Central. Coach Deti had been competing against Central for literally 40 years, since he was in high school. I remember him especially fired up our senior year. He was giving his pre-game speech and spitting all over the guys in the front row. I never remember seeing him so impassioned. Man, he loathed those guys.

I remember vividly being up 21-0 at halftime and as we were walking into the locker room, Coach Deti and the Central coach, Lew Roney, started yelling at each other from across the field. I figured they'd settle down, but they kept getting closer and closer as we walked off the field. Before we knew it they were in each other's faces yelling and screaming, and then someone actually threw a punch--which for a bunch of high school kids it's like the best thing ever to see adults brawl. But we were so shocked we just stood there in silent disbelief.

I am not sure who threw the first punch, but there were several, and a few might have even landed. After that, we all hated Central on a whole new level. I haven't been to a Laramie High-Central football game in almost 25 years, but I know if I went I would be rooting for the good ol' LHS Plainsmen. That's my team.

To me the affinity is strange. How can this abstract notion of a team be so powerful in our lives?

It'll make you do odd things.

The arch nemesis of the University of Wyoming Cowboys (where my father taught) were the Brigham Young University Cougars. We really hated Colorado State, too, since Fort Collins was about an hour from Laramie, but for some reason those Mormons really got under our skin. Probably because so many of them were really nice, really good looking, had good family values--that kind of hatred. The kind that makes no sense.

But they weren't us and that is kind of what mattered. You had your team and they had theirs and never the twain shall meet. Of course the rivalry only mattered, for some reason, in athletics. No one ever cared what was happening in the BYU physics department, but football or basketball was a different story.

When I was in high school, our family went to the conference basketball tournament in Albuquerque, New Mexico. The Cowboys had a pretty good team that year and we expected to meet BYU in the finals. We won the first couple of games and excitement among our fans started to grow. I started to notice more and more gold and brown shirts in the crowd as we entered the arena. We started to say things like "Go Pokes!" and chant "Here we go, Wyo! Here we go!" and high-five complete strangers.

Our collective excitement and support for the team would sometimes take a nasty turn, and eventually someone would begin to taunt our rivals from Utah who had been eliminated in the semi-finals. "BYU, where are youuu?" they would sing out, echoing through the concourse like some crazed yodeler in the Swiss Alps. Sure enough, it would bounce back from another Wyoming fan somewhere in the bowels of the stadium. "BYU, where are youuu?" It was great fun.

When you are part of a group of people, it is amazing how it affects your behavior. You act in a certain way because that is what the group expects.

When your coach starts throwing down with the opposing team, you jump in and throw down. When people from your home state start ridiculous chants at a basketball tournament in New Mexico, you start chanting. It is just what you do.

We were all a thousand miles from home and Wyoming is a small state. There was something pretty cool about seeing people from your neck of the woods so far from home. It was a bonding experience.

Whenever I travel internationally, I am continually amazed at the immediate sense of connection I get with other Americans. Most of these people I have never met and would never have a reason to stop and talk to if we were in the States.

They could be serial killers for all I know. But in a foreign land they are transformed; they are Americans, and that means something. That puts us together, and when you are away from home it is good to have that connection.

I think Peter understands the power of a team, the power of being connected to others, especially for those who are not at home, those who are traveling.

As he wraps up his letter, he offers a few words of encouragement to the veterans, and a few to the rookies. He reminds us that there is an opponent who wants nothing more than to destroy us. Most importantly, perhaps, he reminds us that we are not alone. We have brothers throughout the world who love God, who are fighting the good fight and engaging in the battle with us. So we should endure, we should serve, we should consider others before ourselves.

We are not alone. We have brothers and sisters throughout the world. And that is a good thing to remember.

To Elders Serving *(1 Peter 5:1-4)*

Being the oldest of four boys is both a blessing and curse. A blessing because I got the privilege of doing pretty much everything first: I got to stay up the latest, got the new clothes, got to have friends spend the night and was able to drive before any of my brothers.

It was a curse because, as the eldest, I was given more responsibility, and I was expected to take care of my younger siblings and include them in the things I was doing with my friends.

Now I don't want to say this was all bad all the time. It was nice to always have someone to play with. Someone was always around and you were rarely alone. On the downside, someone was always around and you were rarely alone.

When we began our first trip around the world, I was eleven. Tim (we called him Tad at that point) was ten, Jon was six, and the youngest, Joe, was four. My parents were along for the trip of course, but I do remember feeling a heightened sense of responsibility during that time, kind of like I was in charge.

These kids, my brothers, were vulnerable, weak and frail. And the world is a big, dark, bad place. Who knows what dangers lurk out there? They needed someone to protect them. That's what older brothers are for, of course.

I am not sure I would have been much help at all, had there been any *real* danger, my dad was there for the real trouble, but I think it gave my parents a little more peace of mind knowing I was keeping an eye out for problems.

Peter tells us that the elders, those who are older, are supposed to look out for, to care for, the younger folks in the church. He compares the job to that of a shepherd who keeps an eye on sheep who have a tendency to wander off.

Kind of like my four-year old brother, Joe. Joe was so outgoing and friendly and made friends so quickly that I seriously think my parents' greatest fear was that he would wander into someone's home and fit in so quickly that he would just start thinking they were his family.

I am glad to report that never happened, although there were a lot of Greek grandmothers pinching his cheeks whom I had to keep a pretty close eye on.

It is a really great thing when we have good, well-intentioned older people and leaders looking out for us, for our best interest. On the other hand, I don't know of anything that can more quickly damage or discourage an organization, a family, a group of people, than a leader or elder who has selfish motives.

Peter writes, "Be shepherds of God's flock that is under your care, serving as overseers--not because you must, but because you are willing, as God wants you to be; not greedy for money, but eager to serve; not lording it over those entrusted to you, but being an example to the flock." (5:2-3)

There seem to be two pitfalls that elders may fall into, from Peter's perspective: greed and a lust for power/control.

As an older brother, I can relate to both of those. I could take basically whatever I wanted from my younger brothers; toys, candy, TV remote, bike, whatever. I was bigger and stronger (and better looking I might add) so I used that advantage to get whatever I wanted.

On a similar note, I could also assert my will and make them do what I wanted them to do. I set the agenda, and if what I wanted to do that day was questioned, I had the physical and mental advantage to, again, get what I wanted.

This is many times how businesses, and sometimes churches, operate. The guys in charge make all the money and the decisions. And no one had better get in their way.

My first year playing football in high school, our school had just come off winning the state championship. Most of that team were seniors and had graduated, but a few of the guys who had played were juniors coming back as the top dogs.

The fullback was an all-state, first-teamer named Dane McCoy. Dane was a 6' 1", 230-pound kid who grew up on a ranch about 20 minutes from Laramie. This meant two things: he was solid muscle from lifting hay bales and wrestling cows all the time; and he was fast, probably from having to outrun the bulls.

As the new guys, our job was to play on the scout team against the varsity. We were supposed to mimic the upcoming opponent to give the starters some idea of what they were going to face, both on offense and defense. There was nothing realistic about it.

Most of us had barely reached puberty. Dane had been shaving for probably eight or nine years by then. I think he had a pretty solid IRA as well.

We did our best, but usually Dane had no trouble breaking through the linemen and linebackers, making his way like a crazed ox into the secondary where his only opposition were a few 120-pound, bobble-headed cornerbacks.

Truth be told, we would just turn and run away. No one wants to die on the practice field at Laramie Senior High School.

For some reason, this infuriated Dane; he wanted to run us over. I have no doubt he took great pleasure in inflicting as much pain on us as possible.

And so he would chase us. The guys who should have been hunting him down turned into the hunted. I can still picture little Jeb Westbrook and

Artie Smith sprinting across the golden afternoon prairie as if their lives depended on it, Dane bearing down on them like a wind-driven storm.

I guess the ironic and maybe sad thing is that Dane, for all his talent and physical prowess, failed to understand that these little kids, these younger men, were his teammates. And as the elder, as the leader, the success of the team depended upon his ability to bring us along, to help us be better, to nurture us and to lead by example.

I think we won two games that year.

When elders do not lead with humility, when they are greedy for power and for control, it kills the spirit of the whole team. And everyone loses.

Young Men Clothed *(1 Peter 5:5)*

I think it is hard to travel in a group. For the sake of efficiency and getting stuff done, it is much easier to go alone. But it is also not as fun in many ways. Traveling with your family is great, but there are trade offs.

I had one of the most romantic nights I can remember, strolling the streets of Paris, under the Eiffel Tower, lights awash over the beautiful city. The downside is that I was with my brother Tim. The upside, I wasn't alone, which would have been even more pathetic, maybe.

All that to say, I have done my fair share of traveling both alone and in groups, and while it is more fun to go with a group, it is also much more difficult.

I think this is true for one basic reason: when you travel, you are trying to get somewhere. That is the basic idea of going on a trip. And when you are alone, you get to decide and have the final say in both where and how you go.

This is not so true in a group.

Usually, in a group, the number of opinions and paths to a given destination is directly proportional to the number in the party. Similarly, the level of frustration that said group generates when trying to decide if they should take a taxi, a bus, walk or just sit down and cry outside the airport, is also in direct proportion to the size of said group.

The phrase that comes to mind here is "Too many chiefs, not enough Indians."

Like I said, on our first trip abroad, I was 11. My dad was 43. That worked out well, because there was really no confusion in our little group about who was leading this expedition. (I probably thought I could have done a better job, but he was the one carrying all the money and passports.)

Our job, as the family, was to fall in line behind my dad. And try to keep up. I was usually next in line, then Tim, Jon, Joe and finally my mother, who, being a true servant, stayed in the rear making sure none of us got lost, fell in an open manhole, or wandered off into some alley.

The point is that the whole thing worked pretty well because we lined up behind my dad and he got us to where we were going.

Now, admittedly, as we got older, the balance of power started to shift. On our next trip I was 19. We had shipped our VW bus to Europe, and upon arrival instructed my father that his seat would be the one in the back next to the window where he could "relax" and look out at all the pretty mountains and cathedrals and whatnot.

The boys were taking the lead.

I think we were up to the task, even though Tim started driving on the wrong side of the road when we got off the ferry from England to France.

It was a nervous moment, but he soon righted the ship and we were on our way. We did eventually make it to Hungary. And to my father's credit, he sat in the back and let us take the lead. Probably drove him a bit nuts, but he did it and I think it all worked out fine.

I think Peter knows that in order for the church, for the family of God, to function, people have to be lined up in the right order. And this basically means that the young guys are to line up behind the old guys.

He writes, "Young men, in the same way be submissive to those who are older." The Greek word for "submissive" here is *hupotasso*. It is a military term that means to "line up, arrange yourself under a leader."

I have no idea what would have happened if an 11-year old had decided to go rogue in Singapore, but I am guessing it would not be good.

There is a reason the elders are in the lead.

Things do not always go perfectly, like the time we spent probably close to four hours looking for a hotel in Vienna and finally found one at about one o'clock in the morning. Dad led us to the skankiest hotel in all of Europe, which shall remain unnamed, to protect the innocent and also the author from lawsuit. At least we didn't end up in a gutter. And I give my dad all the credit for that.

I think it bears mentioning that I don't believe Peter is advocating blind allegiance to leaders who are immoral or corrupt, or requiring we violate our conscience with respect to God's laws and directives, or even that we don't push back and offer differing perspectives on a matter. I think great leaders and elders are both teachable and open to rebuke and correction, and I hope would never knowingly abuse those in their charge.

But it happens, and situations like that require much prayer, outside counsel and courage to know the right course. Do I need to line up or is this a case where it is just better to peaceably part ways? Probably nine times out of ten it is a case of just getting in line. We probably bolt too quickly too often, but sometimes it is appropriate to dismiss ourselves from the situation.

Lift You Up *(1 Peter 5:6-7)*

One thing I have noticed when traveling is that there are a lot of people in the world that I have never seen before. I know, I have a very well-developed, keen sense of observation.

A month or so ago I was in southern Brazil visiting my brother Jon. He had been staying by the side of the road about 10 miles from a town called Cacapava.

Before visiting Cacapava, I had never even heard of it. I had no idea that it even existed. And yet here is this town of probably 30 or 40 thousand people in the middle of Brazil. And they are very much like us, they have cars and homes and go to the grocery store. We stopped in a bunch of little shops that could have been right here in the U.S.

I mean this is a normal town with normal people and until a few weeks ago I was just cruising along in my life without a clue.

The whole thing made me feel very small for some reason. I think it is because I gravitate toward the belief that nothing really exists outside of my world, what I see and who I interact with on a daily basis. Certainly nothing important or significant is going on out there.

That's kind of the problem with being a tourist--you start to realize that you are a pretty small person in a pretty big world. There are a lot of people out there, living a lot of interesting lives in a lot of different places.

Like I said, makes me feel a bit insignificant.

And there is something about feeling insignificant that makes you want to be noticed. Maybe the reason we have so many people trying to be famous these days is because there are now more people than ever on our planet. People feel smaller today.

I don't think people in the church are any different. We want to be significant, we want to be noticed. It shouldn't come as a surprise that we have our own cultural celebrities, famous pastors from all over the country and world who are just better than you and me at making a name for themselves. Although, if this book takes off...

I don't want to make blanket judgments because I think most of them have good hearts and really want to help people, but I guarantee more than one has a publicist and a team of PR folks working for them, building their brand.

Peter writes, "All of you, clothe yourself with humility toward one another, because,

'God opposes the proud
but gives grace to the humble.'

"Humble yourselves, therefore, under God's mighty hand, that he may lift you up in due time. Cast all your anxiety on him because he cares for you." (5:5b-7)

What jumps out at me in this short passage is that it says about a million times in three verses that we should humble ourselves, and that if we do, God will lift us up at the right time.

The Greek word for "humble" means to not rise far from the ground. It means to be low, kind of like you are sweeping the floor with your clothes.

It is not a very glamorous stance to be sure. And we usually hire others to sweep up. I do not know too many senior pastors who double as the custodian.

I don't know if it is hard to imagine a life face down in the dirt, or just unpleasant so I block it out, try to pretend it is not possible. It is difficult and stressful to imagine a life where I continually fall on my face (literally or figuratively) in front of others.

I am not sure what kind of life that would be.

Which is I guess why Peter also mentions that we should not be anxious or stressed, but trust that God cares for us *and* that, at the right time, he will lift us up.

A couple things blow my mind about this thought: first, when is the right time, because I am not sure what Jesus is waiting around for; and second, what is it like to be lifted up by God?

I like that God is going to do the lifting. It is exhausting trying to lift myself, trying to make myself important and recognized. I think we have all tried to do that in one way or another. We have done our best to convince people that we are significant and valuable and worth listening to. I am not sure about you, but for me that whole process gets very tiring. I would rather someone else brag on me. Best case scenario, God.

In his letter to the Philippians, Paul writes that because of his humility, God lifted Jesus up to "the highest place and gave him the name that is above every name." (2:9) That's pretty awesome! God is a good publicist if we will let Him do the work, let Him do the lifting up.

I also really like that it will be at the right time, which is, in my opinion, much better than the wrong time. Part of me wishes this was a bit more explicit, such as, "God will lift you up on the third Wednesday of every month," but instead we just get the "Dad" answer: "Don't worry about it. At the right time you will get the credit you deserve." Kind of like the answer I give my daughter when she asks for a hamster. I'll get it for you when I get it for you. Stop asking.

But at the same time, it is a great answer because we know that when we need it, when we need the encouragement, and when we have done our part by being humble, it'll be there. God promises that and that is pretty cool.

Over the years, the best sports teams I was on had one common characteristic: every person on that team cared more about encouraging and supporting and helping each other than themselves. And the results were usually a pretty good team that got lots of recognition in the end. I think that is a little bit of what it is like with God.

Someone to Devour *(1 Peter 5:8-9)*

Last summer I took a trip to Kenya with a good friend of mine to visit the pilot site of Nuru International, a non-profit development organization of which we both serve on the board of directors. After our site visit, John arranged for us to go on a safari to the Masai Mara, a huge, incredible wildlife reserve in southern Kenya.

We stayed at a place called the Royal Mara Resort, which was an open camp in the middle of the reserve. An open camp is one that does not have any fences. This means there are lions and leopards and elephants and, most dangerous, hippos on the loose that could come strolling through the camp and into your tent at any moment.

In fact, there were about 200 hippos that resided in the river just over the small hill from the camp. And apparently they really liked the kind of grass that grew in our little collection of tents.

Another interesting fact I learned while in Africa: hippos kill more people than any other animal in the wild. I hear they are quite territorial, which didn't make me feel much better knowing we were basically sleeping on their dinner table. And if you have ever seen the mouth and jaws of a hippo, it is kind of like a truck trying to swallow you whole. It'd be a bad way to go.

And because our resort thought it would be lousy for business to have guests being eaten by hippos, we had an armed guard assigned to us. Ours was Reagan, a jovial Masai warrior, who carried what looked like about a 140-caliber gun and escorted us everywhere.

I asked him when was the last time he had to use that thing.

"Last week."

"What happened?"

"A hippo was charging. I fired a warning shot, but he kept coming."

"Wow, did you kill it?"

"Yes."

"Do you ever miss?" I asked with some trepidation.

"No. I never miss."

We were in good hands. And thank goodness because the wild is a rough place. And there are lots of things that can and will eat you in a second. Everyone seems really hungry out there.

Every day our guide would take us out to find some wildlife, which usually meant looking for lions, leopards, cheetahs or rhinos. We saw all of those, but maybe the most impressive was also the most gruesome. Funny how that works.

Maybe our second or third morning there we came across about 200 hyenas. Judging from the racket they were making, a very haunting howl/laugh, the sheer numbers and the frenetic activity, it was pretty obvious they had killed something.

It turned out to be a young giraffe. And there wasn't a lot left by the time we got there.

It was really the first time in my life I have seen something that big and beautiful and majestic being devoured. Just ripped to shreds. The violence, the pungent odor, the ripping of flesh was jolting to my senses. It was shocking to say the least. And disturbing.

About 200 yards off, a female giraffe scuttled nervously back and forth, bleating pitifully. I have to assume that she was the mother.

Sometimes I think it takes an experience like that to remember that the world is a rough place. We live pretty sheltered lives in the U.S.; most of the world has to struggle, has to fight to survive.

The ones who forget the danger get eaten.

Peter warns us:

144

"Be self-controlled and alert. Your enemy the devil prowls around like a roaring lion looking for someone to devour. Resist him, standing firm in the faith, because you know that your brothers throughout the world are undergoing the same kind of sufferings." (5:8-9)

We see the carnage around us all the time: murders, wars, famines, children abused, families torn apart by suicides and affairs. Friends betraying friends for a promotion at work. The wealthy taking advantage of the poor. Violence in the streets.

I am not sure who is entirely to blame, whether it is just us, or does Satan shoulder some of that, or all of it? But the world will eat you up. Greed and anger and malice and anxiety. You can be devoured very easily if you are not careful, alert and ready.

And I don't think it is an accident that Peter reminds us that we are not alone in this fight. We have brothers (and sisters) all over the world undergoing the same kind of trials and sufferings that we are.

In Africa, I was told that when zebras are together in a herd, their stripes blend together making it nearly impossible for a predator to focus in on a victim for the kill. However, if one wanders too far from the herd or treks alone, well, it gets ugly.

I take a lot of comfort in knowing that I have people throughout the world trying to keep it together, trying to make it through, trying to live this life of submission and humility and service that Jesus has laid out for us.

There are plenty of days I feel like a lion is gnawing on my ankle or arm. And days like that it's good to remember I am not alone.

Christ Himself *(1 Peter 5:10-11)*

My best friend when I was six was a kid named Scott Worley. Probably the main reason we were friends is that we lived on the same street and neither of us had cars. At that age you are pretty much stuck with what you got.

Scott was a good friend, though. We made forts in the prairie out behind our houses. He was a founding member of the Barrett Street Go-Kart Gang (along with yours truly). We had tons of sleepovers and went to each other's birthday parties for as long as I can remember. He was there in the good times and the bad.

He helped me look for my lost dog a couple of times. We were six. Six year olds don't really have that many "bad" times.

The thing I have noticed about friends is that they tend to come and go, many times based simply on geography. Scott and I never had a falling out, we just aren't around each other any more. I imagine that if we ran into each other we would probably pick up right where we left off, jumping our bikes off little wooden ramps made from plywood and two-by-fours. We might even get the Go-Kart Gang back together.

But chances are, our paths will not soon cross again. I have a lot of friends like that from Wyoming, Ohio, Tennessee and even West Virginia, where I live now. We're still friends, just absentee friends, I guess.

While I am encouraged by Peter's reminder that I have brothers and sisters throughout the world who are enduring the same struggles as me, the reality is that even the closest friends are sometimes gone. No one can be present 24 hours a day, 7 days a week. Those kinds of people are not called friends, they are called stalkers. And you should call the police.

Marriage is probably the closest thing we get to a constant companion, but even then we live most of our lives and face most of our struggles by ourselves. Which is why I think Peter includes the little reminder that Christ Himself is not too far off in all this suffering.

Peter writes, "And the God of all grace, who called you to his eternal glory in Christ, after you have suffered a little while, will himself restore you and make you strong, firm and steadfast." (5:10)

I guess there are a couple things comforting about this. First, that God Himself is going to be strengthening me, making me strong in the midst of suffering and trial. I feel pretty good about that, given that the end game is eternal glory in Christ. Yeah, I can live with that. I used to wish I'd get elected to my high school athletic hall of fame, but eternal glory will suffice.

The second thing that encourages me is a bit more subtle. I feel in Peter's words the proximity, the closeness of God. Maybe I am making assumptions that Peter didn't intend, but it seems to me that to strengthen and restore someone, you have to be close by.

Granted it is God. He can do whatever He wants. He could be sitting in Maui, sipping on one of those fruity umbrella drinks on the beach, strengthening and restoring people everywhere while He orders chicken fingers and curly fries.

That just doesn't seem like Him, though.

Proverbs 18:24 says, "A man of many companions may come to ruin, but there is a friend who sticks closer than a brother."

I am thankful for the company of brothers and sisters God has given me all over the world. I could never overestimate the encouragement they have given me as we travel this road together. I am infinitely more thankful for the companionship of Christ. I am sure I am not alone in that sentiment.

JOIN THE CONVERSATION

Before you read the next chapter stop and read 1 Peter 5:12-13 and share what you think on Twitter at #Strangers&Aliens. I'd love to talk about what jumps out at you.

11 UNTIL THEN
1 Peter 5:12-13

It is hard to overestimate the value of greetings from home when you are traveling. For some reason, a letter from a mother or father about stuff you wouldn't normally listen to for five minutes becomes the most important piece of communication since Lincoln's Gettysburg Address.

The mail came to the Rukum District of western Nepal once a week. If you were lucky. And that assumed someone on the other end was sending you a letter or package, which was not always the case.

I do not remember the actual day, maybe Wednesday, but on mail day I always kept one ear open for the sound of the rickety propeller plane that would make its way over the mountains and down into our little valley.

The weeks you got something from home were really good. The weeks you didn't, well, not so much.

Honestly, it didn't really matter what you got. My mom and dad sent lots of different kinds of information. Usually there was a letter reminding me how boring things were back home (which always cheered me up to some extent, that I was able to escape its clutches).

My father would often send me news from the sports world, usually in the form of a Sports Illustrated that I am sure was current when it was mailed, but out-of-date by a month or two by the time it got to me.

I would devour that thing, reading it from cover to cover. My whole life growing up was riddled with sporting activities, and I think it was the familiarity of seeing football helmets and pads, a basketball, and sweat that reminded me of home. I read every article, even the ones on women's golf, so you know I was pretty desperate for news.

My mother would often send clippings from our local paper, *The Laramie Daily Boomerang*, which has to be in the running for weirdest newspaper names on the planet. It was named after some guy's donkey from what I gather from local lore.

Usually the clippings highlighted some local event or news, which, had I been at home, would have held absolutely no interest. However, 15,000 miles away on the other side of the earth, a glimpse of life in Laramie was inhaled and greatly appreciated.

One summer after college, I ended up in New Guinea overseeing a transition time for the Eastern Highlands Mission. I was all by myself for three months, and the only line of communication I had was an old fax machine. It cost six dollars per piece of paper to send and receive. I also had to fire up a small generator to power the thing (and make sure I had fuel), so scheduling the arrival and departure of a fax was important.

It was a nightmare trying to communicate in that way, but it was worth it to hear from home, to have that pixelated, smudged, curled up paper-bit of connection with my family.

Today it is much easier to stay in touch even from foreign lands, what with the internet and cell phones and the like. A couple of months ago I was on a video call with my parents from a bus in Brazil. They were still in their pajamas having breakfast. It was pretty amazing. More amazing is how annoyed I got when the wi-fi in the bus got a bit sluggish. You'd think I'd be a bit more grateful.

Whatever the mode of communication, the message, if not directly, was subtly two-fold. My parents and family always wanted me to know that they were thinking of me. And second, they always wanted me to know that they were proud of me and that I should keep working hard, keep doing whatever it was that I was doing.

That kind of encouragement goes a long way when you are away from home.

I don't know if Peter was thinking this when he decided to write this letter, this letter that would eventually find its way into our hands today, but the effect has to be the same. When you are a traveler, it is good to hear from home. It is encouraging.

I doubt humans felt that much different about things back then as we do now.

Stand Fast *(1 Peter 5:12)*

My first year of organized football was in seventh grade at Laramie Junior High School. Our family had just returned from our year in the jungle in New Guinea; this was a new school and I felt like a new kid just moving into town.

I went out for football because I loved to play football, but on some level I think I was trying to fit in and forge an identity for myself as well.

The Dunham boys matured late in life and in seventh grade I was about 4'10" and probably weighed close to 105 pounds. There were a few others about that size but I was easily in the bottom five percent.

On the other end of the scale were guys like T.J. Barilla. Five foot nine, he clocked in at about 185. I swear to you that kid had to shave twice a day. He was an animal. T.J. was all-world in seventh grade. He was our tailback and I don't think he got tackled all year. Seventh graders bouncing off him like bugs off the windshield of a semi-truck.

It was quite a wake-up call going from touch football in the park to full-speed, full- pads tackle football. I ain't gonna lie: getting run over hurts. But what was even tougher was the prospect of going through all that pain and not getting a chance to play in the games.

I was trying out for the quarterback position, mostly because I figured that was the place you were least likely to get run over. Your job was basically to hand the ball to T.J. It was also the most glamorous position, and from what I could tell you had a good shot of getting a girlfriend and winning the respect of classmates if you could secure that job.

The only problem was that Justin Dowler was also trying out for quarterback. I don't remember him being much bigger or faster, but he was getting all the reps in practice with the first team. I was running scout team which mostly entailed me hanging on to T.J. like a scared mosquito as he dragged me and about eight other guys across the prairie.

Things did not look good for me to get the starting QB nod.

To make matters worse, I found out that Justin's uncle was a two-time Super Bowl champion with the Green Bay Packers, Boyd Dowler. He might be in the Hall of Fame now. Things were really not looking good.

So I did what any normal person would do in that situation. On the ride home from practice one night, I turned to my dad said, "I'm going to quit football."

"What?!" he said, my proclamation obviously taking him off guard. Dad had never quit anything in his whole life and he had even been born without a left pectoral muscle. (Just making sure you remembered. Annoying, huh?)

"I'm going to quit. Justin Dowler is going to get to be the quarterback and I can't beat him. His uncle was in the Super Bowl!"

"You're not going to quit." came the reply.

"Why not?" The old man was not getting it.

"You're not going to quit, because you're a Dunham and Dunhams don't quit."

I don't remember if I said anything at that point. Knowing me, I probably just got irritated, but in hindsight I appreciate what he did for me in that moment.

I do not think this is unlike Peter's last few words of encouragement to us. He writes, "With the help of Silas, whom I regard as a faithful brother, I have written to you briefly, encouraging you and testifying that this is the true grace of God. Stand fast in it." (5:12)

I think Peter is referring back to his entire letter, but maybe specifically the part he had just written when he says this is the true grace of God. What he just wrote is "the God of all grace, who called you to his eternal glory in Christ, after you have suffered a little while, will himself restore you and make you strong, firm and steadfast." (5:10)

I think what he means is that he wants to encourage us not to quit, to keep going, because we belong to God, we have His name, and He is not going to let us quit. He's going to keep us going even though it can be kind of miserable now.

My dad was not going to let me quit because he knew that quitting was not good for me. I think our heavenly Father is the same kind of Dad. He's not going to let us quit; He's going to empower us to overcome, to endure, to hang in there. And He is going to send people like Peter and Paul and my dad and scores of others to encourage us to keep going until we finally get home.

Those were good words my father spoke to me in that car on the way home from football practice. Words I still remember and that still encourage me to this day.

God himself will restore you and make you strong, firm and steadfast. This is the true grace of God. Stand fast in it.

Greetings *(1 Peter 5:13)*

Writing letters is kind of a lost art. I don't mean emails, I mean the kind where you sit down, take out a piece of paper and a pen and write.

I cannot remember the last time I wrote that kind of letter, a letter to just say hi, to just let someone know I was thinking of them. I guess we do that kind of thing with text and twitter and Facebook nowadays.

I mentioned this before, but my dad asked my mom to marry him while the two drove back to Michigan from New York about three months after they met. He was just lying down for a nap in the back seat. She wisely said no and kept driving.

But my father is stubborn and a writer and I guess he knew the power of the pen. So he started to send her letters once he returned to school in Arkansas and she went to work in Traverse City, Michigan.

I think he wrote her everyday. I have no idea what you would write about everyday, but it was probably scintillating stuff like, "Today I went to the grocery store and bought tea!" or "Summertime in Little Rock is very hot and humid. LOL." Except they didn't have LOL back then. They probably didn't even laugh to themselves. The '60s were a serious and turbulent time.

I am pretty sure he was stalking her, but people were less wary of weirdos in those days and the funny thing is that those letters worked. She actually married the guy that December.

Which now that I think about it is a good thing.

Mom says that God just kept moving in her heart that she should marry Dad, which I take to mean it took an act of God for her to marry him, but whatever.

I think she admired his persistence and it had to be nice to know that someone was thinking about you every single day. Creepy, but nice.

Every few weeks a letter to my daughter will come in the mail. It is usually covered in stickers of cats and smiley faces and the like. Inside there is a letter written on purple or pink or rainbow stationery, in big, grade school handwriting a short, simple letter. Usually the questions are of the sort, "How are you? Did you get a new kitten yet? Are you going to Canada with your dad?"

Probably because she rarely gets mail, Grace is always surprised to find one addressed to her. She absolutely lights up when she sees her name on the envelope and she always says the same thing:

"I wonder who this could be from?"

But I think she knows. It is from her grandmother who lives sometimes in Ohio, sometimes in Wyoming, but is always thinking about her grandchildren.

It is so good to know that someone, somewhere is thinking of you. And that simple piece of paper or email or text or tweet goes a long way, much further than the distance it had to travel to reach you.

It is the thought of home, but mostly of the love and support and the hope of one day reconnecting with friends and family, that most encourages the heart of the traveler.

Peter ends his letter letting us know that "the one who is in Babylon, chosen together with you, sends you her greetings, and so does my son Mark." (5:13)

It is a little weird on first glance that the woman "in Babylon" is not named. Apparently, Peter knew that they would know who he was talking about.

And maybe he knew that we would be reading this a couple thousand years later on a journey of our own, and he just wanted us to remember that someone, one who cares, who loves you but is not with you, and maybe is away in Babylon, or Ohio or California or Africa or wherever, is thinking of you.

That person sends their greetings. They are thinking of you. They are praying for you that you will hang in there as you travel, as you are away from home, and what is more, away from them, and they cannot wait to see you again. I think that one of the greatest things about heaven, about finally getting home, is that we will be reunited with the people we love. Certainly that includes those who have gone before us, have passed away, and have been physically absent from our lives.

But I believe it will be so much more than that; I think it will be a spiritual reunion as well, that all Christians will be reconnected when the veil of sin and pain and misunderstanding and distrust and hurt that divides us in this life is taken away as we are gathered in the presence of Christ. We will see each other more clearly then, without the distorting effects of this world; we will all pass through and meet anew on the other side.

JOIN THE CONVERSATION

There is so much more that Peter talks about than I could ever discuss in a single book. And I am sure that you have had observations that I totally missed. Please share your thoughts on Twitter at #Strangers&Aliens. I'd love to talk with you more about 1 Peter. It is a rich book.

CONCLUSION

At the beginning of this book I started telling you that a couple weeks ago Grace and I took a camping trip to Canada. She had been dying to go. After all, that is the dream of most nine-year olds.

So we packed up my old Chevy Blazer and headed north through Pittsburgh and up to Niagara Falls, through Toronto and into Ontario.

Immediately upon crossing the border, you realize you are no longer at home. All the speed limit signs are in kilometers. Speed limit 110, are you serious? That's awesome! Oh wait, that's like 34 miles per hour. (The conversion thing was tough until I realized my speedometer actually *has* the KPH equivalents on it.)

We made our way around Lake Ontario, and stayed at Darlington and Sandbanks Provincial Parks our first couple nights. Incredible views of the lake and beautiful dunes. It is a wonder the Canadians are so nice with the onslaught of bugs they have to endure. Massive mosquitos and nasty, biting horse flies. Maybe that is what keeps them from exploding with joy and glee.

We spent most of our time in Quebec, which I sensed is proudly Canadian, but also pretty pumped to speak French (or Quebecois, which to the high school-trained ear sounds *exactly* like what I think French sounds like).

Everything was in French, even the instructions on the gas pump, which seems downright un-American to me, but whatever, it's a free country. At least I think so.

Canada is maybe the least scary foreign country I have been to, but still there is some anxiety when you don't know the language (with apologies to Mrs. Kirkwood who tried her best for three years of French class) and really don't know where you are going.

As you know by now, it is an unwritten rule in our family that Dunhams do not make reservations for lodging when on an exploratory/adventure trip. The key advantage of this policy is flexibility. If we find something or someplace cool we are not forced to move on because of a despotic reservation. (It just occurred to me that we could always cancel the reservation, but there are penalties and the hassle, and well, it just violates the *principle* of it all.)

The downside is that you often find yourself getting on in the evening with no place to stay. That can cause some stress. We like to call it adventure.

Many times in my life I feel like I do not know what I am doing or where I am going. Am I in the right job? Am I making the most of my time and talents? What in the world am I supposed to be doing? Where should I be headed?

It feels very much like traveling to Canada, hoping to find a place to stay for the night. You wonder what you are going to find, if there is a place for you.

Three times during this trip, Grace and I pulled into a provincial or national park hoping to find a place. And three times, at Darlington and Sandbanks Provincial Parks and at La Mauricie National Park, we were informed that there was one single remaining campsite in the entire area.

Three times. Three times we got the last place. Three times we looked at each other and shook our heads in disbelief. (I actually watched as they turned away the cars behind me. This was not a feel-good marketing ploy or a passive-aggressive attempt at telling me to book ahead next time, which you might reasonably assume.)

I hate to over-spiritualize things, and I could easily write this whole episode off as a coincidence, but I couldn't help but believe that God was trying to tell me something. 99.99% of the time there are no more campsites when I roll into town. For this to happen three times in one trip was way beyond an accident in my mind.

I think God was telling me, up there in Canada, that He has a place for me, a place with Him and He is guiding me, guiding us, leading us and providing for us along the way until we get home to Him.

My life is full of doubt and uncertainty. It is full or strangeness and a deep sense that I don't really live here, this is not my home. And because of that I know there is another new and different way, a different life to be lived out there somewhere.

And all this feels like a journey, a path laid out by someone bigger and wiser and with a far better perspective than mine. Filled with pain and disappointment and struggle and joy and peace and laughter and tears. I know I am on my way home. I am on my way to God.

TREY DUNHAM

158

ABOUT THE AUTHOR

Trey Dunham is from Wyoming, the son of a college professor and a mother who ran around looking after four boys. He grew up in a conservative Baptist church, but did not really get on board with Jesus until moving to Budapest, Hungary in 1989. He has lived around the world, from the jungles of New Guinea to the Himalayas of Nepal to the eastern BLOC during the fall of communism. He has a bachelor's degree in philosophy from Denison University and a doctorate from West Virginia University. Trey has been a Bible teacher for more than a decade and currently lives in Morgantown, WV with his daughter, Grace. *Strangers & Aliens* is his first anecdotal commentary.

You can follow him on Twitter @TreyDunham
or on his website, TreyDunham.com.

Made in the USA
Lexington, KY
02 August 2013